Cathy Lechner

I'M TIRED OF CRYING, IT'S TIME TO LAUGH AGAIN!

Cathy Lechner

I'M TIRED OF CRYING, IT'S TIME TO LAUGH AGAIN!

Charisma®
HOUSE

I'M TIRED OF CRYING, IT'S TIME TO LAUGH AGAIN!
by Cathy Lechner
Published by Charisma House
A part of Strang Communications Company
600 Rinehart Road
Lake Mary, Florida 32746
www.charismahouse.com

Unless otherwise noted, all Scripture quotations are from the New King James Version of the Bible. Copyright © 1979, 1980, 1982 by Thomas Nelson, Inc., publishers. Used by permission.

Scripture quotations marked KJV are from the King James Version of the Bible.

Cover and interior design by Pat Theriault

Library of Congress Catalog Card Number: 2001087273
International Standard Book Number: 0-88419-753-0

02 03 04 05   8 7 6 5 4 3 2
Printed in the United States of America

Dedication

For my darling brothers

Steven Lind Rothert

and

Harold Randall Rothert

You make my life so joyous—

I could never imagine

my world without you.

Acknowledgments

No book is ever written without help, not even the Bible! So it gives me tremendous delight to publicly acknowledge and say "thank you" to all those who continually put their life on hold to help me.

To my ever faithful and hard-working mother, Rose—She tells people we get along really well. She says, "She tells me what to do, and I do it." That pretty well sums it up. You are incredible, Mom! If my own children love, honor and respect me as much as your children and grandchildren love you, I will feel fulfilled.

To Erin—She is much more than my secretary, she is my best friend. There is something to be said about one who said she would never leave...and didn't. Is loyalty such a difficult thing? I suppose so. Thank you, Erin.

To my hard-working, always compliant, daughter Jerusha—You cheer for all my crazy plans and then jump in to make sure they get done. I don't know how God is going to give you a husband who will be worthy enough.

To Hannah, Gabriel, Samuel, Abagael, Lydia and Hadassah—You are just now becoming aware of what your mommy does and how important it is. I love it that you think we are all famous.

To my man, Randi—Here's to the next twenty-five years, Sweetheart. I'm willing if you are!

To Ann, Thelma, Michelle, Paulette, Unita—Each has contributed because she believes in the vision God has entrusted to me. It's a good thing I don't have to pay each of you, because I wouldn't have enough money.

To my new poodle, "Pee Oui"—You are only three months old and weigh only two pounds, so your contribution to the book consists of sitting on my lap. But come on, everybody—he is incredibly cute!

To my precious Jesus—It would be demeaning to try to put what we share into words. I love You!

CONTENTS

CHAPTER 1

AN OPEN HEAVEN—A LAVISH GOD

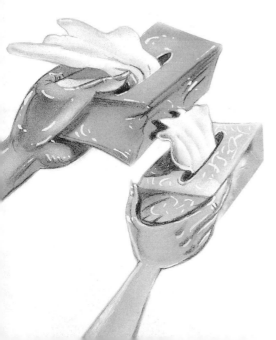

Her gorgeous face was covered with sweet tears as she brushed back her beautiful thick, black hair. One could sense that the emotion she was feeling at this moment overwhelmed her.

I was a long way from home—literally on the other side of the world—sitting in a restaurant high above Sydney's famous Darling Harbor. Taking advantage of our window seats, I leaned toward the window and looked out, not really seeing anything. You see, a small miracle was taking place at that little restaurant table. That's how awesome our God is!

Life was going on all around us, and right in the middle of it all, God showed up and did what I call "a quiet miracle."

The beautiful young woman sitting across from me was the wife of the pastor of a very successful and growing church. The previous night I'd had the honor of ministering at their church, and we had a wild God time. I had met these pastors during my previous trips to Australia, but I had never had the opportunity to fellowship with them before. Of course, fellowship is the Christian code word for *eating*.

The Spirit of God really drew me to her. In the natural, I refuse to stand next to a 5-foot 10-inch, 115-pound, gorgeous woman. While I am certainly not blaming my parents, who after seeing me still decided to keep me, I reached my top height at fifteen years of age. Essentially, when I stood beside this woman, her legs started at about my shoulder. Her long, thick, black hair, even when messed up, simply looked windblown. Oh, the inequities of life! But I agreed to have lunch with her. She was to pick me up at my hotel, and we would spend some quality time fellowshiping, that is, eating.

The night before we were to meet, I was in my hotel

room when suddenly I felt impressed by the Holy Spirit to buy this new friend a gift. It was to be a kiss from God, a sort of "thank you" from the Lord to her. Since it was a gift from my heart, I knew just what to buy. It would be a beautiful French leather handbag. It was something I was certain she would not buy for herself. She was the mother of four, a pastor's wife and very sensible.

When she arrived to take me to lunch, I asked her if we could possibly stop by the French Leather Purse store. To be extremely polite, and taking into consideration the fact that I had no basic understanding of this major downtown business and world commerce center, she said, "Sure, but I'll circle the block until you are finished, and then I'll come back for you."

I knew that just wouldn't do. How could I possibly buy an expensive, personal gift for someone I barely knew if she wasn't present? I insisted that she park the car and come in with me. She was very polite, but let me know that parking spaces were almost nonexistent at lunchtime in downtown Sydney. I grudgingly acquiesced and hopped out of the car at the corner.

As soon as I walked into the store, I knew I wasn't at my local Wal-Mart back in Florida. The handbags were in lighted cases, locked up behind a counter. How could I choose? What if my purchase ended up being some horrible gift? Would she smile politely, thank me and then go bury it in the backyard? Even the store personnel seemed to sense that I did not belong there. One well-meaning saleslady offered to show me the scarf section, which is priced three levels below belts and watch fobs.

Just as I was about to ask if they had a "seconds" department, I heard a cheery "hi" behind me. My new friend told me that the most incredible thing had

3

happened just after she had dropped me off. As she rounded the corner, a man standing beside a Range Rover jumped in his car as he waved my friend into the parking space. She said it was as if he had been holding the spot directly in front of the store just for her.

What a God we serve! I guess the angels drive Range Rovers. This was beginning to be a very exciting day. I loved the thought that she was helping me choose a handbag for herself.

WE HAVE AN EXTRAVAGANT GOD.

A sales associate suddenly appeared, he himself being imported from France to sell overpriced handbags made from extremely expensive cows.

Then suddenly, we saw IT—a gorgeous, black bucket shoulder bag. After I signed away both kidneys and an ovary, he unlocked the case and laid, no, presented the purse on a background of black velvet. I got the distinct impression that this gentleman really enjoyed selling ladies' purses—perhaps a little too much.

"Voilà," he said as he proceeded to tell us what a remarkable choice we had made. It was the newest thing out, and I think it was the most expensive handbag in the world. It was absolutely gorgeous. I asked my friend to model it for me. It was perfect. I will admit that my heart almost stopped and I felt as if a lump the size of a grapefruit stuck in my throat when I was told that the price was equivalent to the budget of feeding two small nations for a month. Oh well, the

4

transaction was completed and we were on our merry way to eat, that is, fellowship.

Dessert, which is mandatory for U.S. citizens, was served after our lovely meal, and then the table was cleared. I had safely tucked under the table "the bag," which had been gloriously wrapped by the swishy guy. I brought it in under the pretense that someone might steal it if I left it in the car.

A KISS FROM AN EXTRAVAGANT GOD

The look on her face was a moment in time that will remain in my mind forever. It must be the look that God got when He saved us, or when He opened that proverbial door that no man can close.

As I put the package on the table, she had that deer-in-the-headlights look.

"It's for you."

"I...I...can't...it's just too, too..."

"Extravagant!" I yelled out. "It's much too extravagant. But we have an extravagant God."

She didn't protest, and she didn't argue. She just wept beautiful, lovely, joyous tears. In an instant this gesture went from being a really nice gift for a friend of mine to a huge kiss from her Father.

You know, the Word is filled with words that describe our God, words like *awesome, great and mighty, wonderful, beautiful, gracious* and *merciful*, just to name a few. We don't get extravagant gifts every day, but once in a while, God will surprise us with His goodness.

She touched the bag. She held it up to her face so she could smell the new leather. To further surprise her, I had bought a little hook-in bag to put inside the purse. Weeping openly, she said, "No one has ever

5

done anything like this for me."

She then began to pour out about all the wilderness seasons she had experienced over the past seven or more years. I was surprised, but not disappointed, to hear that she had been married before. Her first husband had been a bodybuilder, and she had been a swimsuit model. Can you believe it? A swimsuit model! I have serious problems being best friends with

I NOW REALIZE WHY GOD WANTED TO THROW THIS GIRL A PARTY. HE LOVED HER.

a swimsuit model. Her first pregnancy resulted in the birth of twin boys and a hundred-pound weight gain. (There *is* a just God!)

When her babies were three weeks old, her wonderful, Christian, pastor-husband-at-the-time, walked out and left her for another woman. Her self-esteem nosedived, her ministry was left in tatters, and she had her world turned upside down.

By the grace of God, she had hung in there with her Lord, and He didn't disappoint her. Just a couple of years later, He sent her a man of God with a heart of compassion I have rarely seen. He brought a beautiful daughter into their union, and now together they copastor one of the most exciting churches in the city. Awesome! And along with all that, God gave them a precious baby girl of their own together.

HE IS FAITHFUL

Precious friend, that is the character of our faithful God. Many Christians are in servitude to a God I don't recognize. He is angry, disappointed and stingy. He meagerly hands out miniscule blessings, but only after much begging and pleading. I think the sin of the children of Israel was that they offended God by misjudging His character. "Yes, again and again they tempted God, and limited the Holy One of Israel" (Ps. 78:41).

I now realize why God wanted to throw this girl a party. He loved her. He appreciated her. He was grateful that she continued to trust Him and believe His Word that declared she would live to see His goodness in the land of the living. I had the privilege of being a part of this incredible demonstration of His heart toward her.

I know, it was only a purse, but it was the best purse. It only represented a tiny portion of His infinite compassion when He thinks of us.

Now for those of you who might think me wasteful, let me explain. I am not wealthy. We are responsible for seven children and a staff of ten. In reality, I had to use my Visa card because I didn't have that much money. One would say it could have been used in other "religious" streams. We could have bought Bibles and smuggled them into China or had tracts dropped from a plane over Russia. But instead, through this act of love, God broke the alabaster box over my precious friend.

Back in the hotel, I began rehearsing what I would say to my husband when the Visa bill arrived. I knew it would eventually find its way back to my house in Jacksonville. After coming up with a few different scenarios, I decided that honesty was best.

Then just before I left for home, someone surprised me by putting in my hand a sum of money that amounted to the exact cost of the purse, including the tithe on the amount. Isn't that just like our God? How awesome is that?!!

After being back home for a week, I was still experiencing a really bad case of jet lag. I was committed to a meeting in Daytona Beach, so I had to go in spite of how I was feeling. After the meeting, I got in my car, and there on the front seat was a beautifully wrapped box (as opposed to the recycled paper and bows that *some* people use).

It wasn't my birthday, anniversary or any major gift-requiring day. To my absolute elation, I lifted the box top and pulled back the tissue paper to reveal…guess what? That's right, the very same handbag I had admired in a store not many days prior.

Now it was my turn to weep.

CHAPTER 2

AN EXTRAVAGANT GOD—JESUS DOESN'T HAVE TO WEAR A MUUMUU

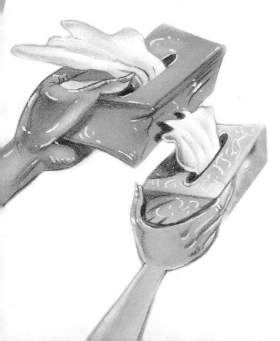

I spend a lot of time in airports. Not really by choice, but by call and appointment.

Anyone who has ever traveled can attest to the wearing down of every nerve in your body as the three-year-old seated behind you keeps latching and unlatching the tray table attached to the back of your seat. Which, I might add, is usually the middle seat in the next to the last row.

Usually there is a very, very large, hairy man seated on the aisle who falls asleep while the plane is sitting on the runway waiting for the Second Coming.

Knowing I can't get up because the seat belt light is on seems to trigger a mechanism in my bladder that makes it necessary for me to get up every ten minutes.

When the millennium eventually does come and you actually take off, the large, hairy man has drifted sideways with his mouth hanging open so that drops of drool from his bottom lip are now falling on your shoulder.

I've listened to all the great guys like Jesse Duplantis, Kenneth Copeland and awesome women of God whom I adore, and they all have great airplane stories. Either the plane they were about to take crashed after God told them not to get on it, or they witnessed about the Lord to the entire plane, and four Jehovah Witnesses, a Buddhist and a pair of Tibetan monks got saved.

My problem is this: I imagine that every plane I'm scheduled to fly on is the one I'm not supposed to take, but I go anyway. I really try to strike up a conversation and witness, but my seatmates usually just nod at me and then close their eyes as they put on their headphones.

I have finally come to the conclusion that travel is part of the pressure and the plan and sometimes the pain in my life. Actually, I really do hear from God when I am traveling. In fact, right there in 34B, God speaks.

As difficult as air travel can be, with its delayed flights, canceled flights or traveling with the entire eighth-grade girls volleyball team, it's still always worth it when I finally reach my destination.

What an awesome God-principal that is in our lives. Oh yes, it's a hard and sometimes lonely journey. And yes, you're tired, but then so are a lot of us. But the end result is always wonderful. As I get older, I find myself wanting the journey to be easier, but apparently God thinks exactly the opposite. Isn't that a great thought?

SEEING FROM A FRESH PERSPECTIVE

One time someone sent me a brand-new Bible. It had my name engraved on the front. It was still in the box and smelled like new, simulated, porcupine leather. The pages had never been opened, so I left it in the box.

Bibles are not like anything else you own, and I own several. My first little blue Bible had a zipper cross, and I carried to VBS and church (that is, when I remembered to take it).

13

Then there is my old green hardback Living Bible my parents gave me. It is lovingly inscribed with my maiden name. I remember getting it as a gift when I graduated from high school in 1972.

In my nightstand beside my bed is my grandfather's Bible. He died when I was five, so my memories of him are vague. I mostly remember him when I look into my Uncle Joe's face. My grandparents came from Sicily and couldn't read English, so his Bible is in the Italian language.

My preaching Bible lost its semi-Naugahyde leather

smell about eight years ago. Pieces of Exodus and James are missing because one time I broke the binding shoving the poor thing into my hanging bag. I have nicer Bibles, but one in particular has my heart.

WHAT AN AWESOME GOD-PRINCIPLE— IT'S STILL ALWAYS WORTH IT WHEN WE FINALLY REACH OUR DESTINATION.

After my father died, I asked my mother for only one of his possessions—his Bible. When she gave it to me, it still had a stack of my dad's sermons tucked into the cover. Closing my eyes, I can still picture my daddy with that Bible on his lap. I can see it opened up on the pulpit as he preached with a great anointing that I could only hope for. But alas, it also stays in the drawer.

As usual, I had procrastinated, and at the last minute I began packing for a weekend of ministry. As I was feverishly throwing clothes, shoes, makeup and sermon notes into my luggage, I discovered that I couldn't find my preaching Bible.

I was running late and was trying to get out the door while six little tear-stained faces were crying, hanging on to my leg and moaning…and I couldn't find my Bible.

I panicked and looked everywhere I thought it might be. I could not imagine having to preach without my

14

well-worn, precious Bible. I knew where all my favorite scriptures were in it. It would immediately open to my most-read chapters because I had been there so many times before. My eyes knew instinctively where to look on the page to find the verse I wanted. Besides, it was also a large-print edition. Everyone knows that the older you get, the smaller they print the letters.

But I could wait no longer; I had to leave. With much reluctance, I opened the box that contained the leather, fragrance-enhanced, new Bible and put it in my suitcase.

Have you ever made hasty judgements about someone based on how worn his (or her) Bible was when you glanced over at it? No? Well, I guess I'm the only one then. I was actually embarrassed by this new Bible, with its new pages sticking together. I thought I could hear the pastor and his wife looking at me and quietly having this conversation:

Pastor Flinley: "My, Cathy has a very new Bible."

Mrs. Pastor: (Looking at me suspiciously.) "I saw it. It doesn't look as though she has ever used it."

Pastor Flinley: "You are right, dear. Probably never even read it."

Together: (With a withering glare.) "Hmmm!"

Do you think I am oversensitive?

Later, when I was safely hidden in my hotel room, I tried to rough up my new Bible. I remembered hearing a visiting missionary say that there were whole nations who had to share two pages of a Bible that had been smuggled in by a bush pig farmer. And here I was, slamming my Bible around so people would think I was spiritual. It was really sort of funny to see.

Then the most wonderful thing happened to me in that hotel room. As I leafed through those pages, I began to see scriptures that, for some mysterious reason, were

15

not in my old Bible. Of course, they were always there, but it took a new book to give me a fresh look.

YOUR LOVING LORD WANTS TO SHOW YOU HOW TO MOVE YOUR EYES AWAY FROM YOUR "THINGS" AND TO THE INCREDIBLE DOOR THAT IS OPEN FOR YOU IN HEAVEN.

As I read Revelation 4, the words literally leaped off the pages to me. I have honestly never been a great reader of the Book of Revelation, which is actually odd since the prophetic is where God uses Randi and me.

Visions of beasts, multiheaded demons, a really, really cranky woman who is PMSing—all this does not make for easy reading. I would rather dwell in the Psalms and Samuel, and hang around Corinthians for a while. And who doesn't just *love* Malachi?

AFTER THESE THINGS...

However, there in bold print, right before my eyes, God was speaking to my heart. *"After these things I looked, and behold, a door standing open in heaven"* (Rev. 4:1). It really got my attention because I had been seeking the Lord for some personal needs.

16

It isn't my intention to get all weird and spooky-spiritual, but at times the Lord uses very simple things to let us know He loves us, that He is for us and that we're on the right track.

My old, faithful preaching Bible was also a file folder for some sentimental possessions. One of these was a picture, with a memorial write-up, of my late father. Wherever I went, I would take Daddy, too. Many times I lovingly touched his face in the picture and told him I still loved him and missed him so much. My new Bible was empty of such sorrowful reminders...things.

"After these things..." We all have things. They may be wonderful things like salvation, baptism, our marriage and the birth of a child. Or these things may be painful memories like a divorce, the passing of a loved one, a failure or being disappointed with what life has handed us.

"Hey, I'm talking to YOU!" That's right. I'm talking to you, the one who isn't even sure if God hears you anymore; you, the one who says that if He does hear you, He's not doing anything for you.

"After these things I looked..." Your loving Lord wants to show you how to move your eyes away from your "things" and to the incredible door that is open for you in heaven.

By the way, my mother taught us many rules of etiquette. She did not want three rebellious kids breaking her heart. Her rules included these:

1.　Never take the first of anything or the last of anything on the dinner table— your father may want it.

2.　Never go into someone else's house or room without knocking.

17

3.   Never, ever go into someone else's refrigerator without asking his permission.

Of course, there were about 27,853 more of Mom's rules of life, give or take a few. My brothers and I have passed on most of these rules to our own children.

HIS OPEN DOOR TO US

There is one exception to her Rule #2. On Thursday mornings, I have a prayer meeting in my home from 10 A.M. to 11 A.M. These awesome intercessors have access to my home. I unlock the door and go back in the family room to pray. People arrive and slip in and out during that hour.

That, my friend, is an open door. I can feel the excitement even as I pen this manuscript. I marvel at the fact that God has His door open to us. All of heaven is at our disposal, and if we don't enter in, it is not God's fault— it is our problem. Sadly, many Christians are still pounding on the door. Hey! It's open. Come on in.

I don't believe John was merely describing heaven as a place where we go when we die. I believe the kingdom of God is where all of our needs are met—it's a place of access to our Daddy.

Coming from a Sicilian family, we are very affectionate. I can remember visiting our grandparents when I was a child. As soon as we entered the house, we were instructed to go and kiss "Nana," then "Nonu." If any of the aunts or uncles were there, we kissed them, too. Respect for our elders was vitally important.

When we left, the same ritual was followed. We made the rounds of giving all of the family a kiss. We did the same when we went to bed at night. It was so comforting and sweet.

When our family got together (i.e. to eat), everyone would be talking at the same time, hands flying, voices raised, all with much laughter. It's what I call *orderly chaos*. If nine people were sitting around the kitchen table (where everyone loved to gather), there would be five conversations all going on at the same time.

ALL OF HEAVEN IS AT OUR DISPOSAL, AND IF WE DON'T ENTER IN, IT IS NOT GOD'S FAULT—IT IS OUR PROBLEM.

The first time I brought my new husband to one of these gatherings, he looked at me incredulously and said, "How can you stand this?" He had come from a very disciplined military home, so he was amazed at all the noise and confusion and the open affection we liberally displayed, all of which gave us comfort and security.

19

I have trained my children to greet their grandmother with a kiss whenever she visits us or when they visit her. We honor her for her wisdom and strength (and age, but don't tell her).

People who come from nonaffectionate families and then enter into Charismatic churches are often surprised when a stranger runs up to them, grabs them and squeezes their guts or plants a kiss on their cheeks.

RUN TO THE FATHER AND KISS HIM

When you come into the Father's house, run to Him, kiss Him and show Him honor. So many times the first thing we do when we run into Father's house is weep, make demands and throw our needs in His face. What kind of a reception is that for our heavenly Father?

TWO-THIRDS OF YOUR BATTLE IS MAKING THE DECISION TO "COME UP HERE."

If you will simply come through the open door, the open heaven, and first greet our Father with a kiss, He who loves us will kiss us in return (Song of Sol. 1).

We come to the most holy throne room. I liken it to coming home, but it's our Father's house.

I love to lie on the floor with my babies and play tickle belly with them, pulling up their little shirts and blowing on their soft tummies. That desire to love our children was put into us by God. We have His nature.

We show Him honor and respect when we push past the distracting "things," come boldly unto the throne of grace and kiss the Father. During our worship time, His joy overflows in us. We laugh, we cry, we even fall on the floor. If that isn't the Father playing tickle belly, I don't know what is!

"Come up here, and I will show you things which must

take place" (Rev. 4:1). Take note of the fact that two-thirds of God's name is GO. His nature is bringing us higher from glory to glory and from faith to faith.

There are things we will never receive unless we "*come up here.*" Instead we would like Him to come down to where we are. We say something like, "I'm the one in the muumuu with stringy hair, sitting on the couch eating candy."

Think about it: Two-thirds of your battle is making the decision to "*come up here.*"

CHAPTER 3

A VESSEL OF HONOR OR A KNICKKNACK WAITING TO BE DUSTED?

Many of us have had the opportunity to travel to a foreign country as part of a ministry team. On occasion a friend of mine will send me a letter—four pages, single-spaced—outlining her (or his) ministry. The letter will explain that "the call" to evangelize and win the lost in "Zerggoseta Vaha" began when she was a three-month-old fetus. She is ecstatic. For ten days next spring, she will have the opportunity to fulfill her calling.

Now this is where I, a friend of the ten-day missionary, come in. She wants to give me the opportunity to send her money to help her go. I have chance to help send her so that *I* won't have to go there myself. After all, who wants to go to a mosquito-infested land, eat bugs' eyes and sleep in a house that is overrun with rats and has no electricity?

Now don't misunderstand me. I have done all that many times myself. It's no picnic. I do actually find it much easier to send my letter-writing friends an offering and tell them that I'll be standing with them in prayer. However, please allow me to admonish you...I don't do this with every letter I get, so drop your pen!

Because these weekend missionaries are eternally grateful for my ten-dollar offering, they feel moved to bring me a small thank-you gift for my sacrifice. Twenty minutes before their airplanes take off, they frantically head for the market where little pieces of native stuff (i.e. junk) can be bought for a fraction of what I would pay for them at Wal-Mart.

I fumble for words, "Oh, thank you, it's just so... so...well, I don't even know what to say. God bless you. You really didn't have to..." I don't really want to lie or say what I think, but I get as close as I can.

"No, no, no...no need to thank me," my temporary missionary friend reassures me. "I wanted to bless you. I'm so grateful that you responded to my letter." If I were to be quite honest with my friend, I would tell her that I could very well have waited until eternity and the great judgment day to receive my reward. But what could I say?

So instead, I take the napkins, tablecloth, wooden spoon, trivet or entrails-splaying device and add it to my collection of thank-you gifts from other missionaries, TBN memorabilia and a vast assortment of must-have items that once lined the twenty-five-hundred hospitality gift baskets given to the guest speaker—me. This hodgepodge can be divided into categories like prayer, praise, travel and tacky.

Allow me to digress a moment. Please know that I appreciate all the lovely articles that different groups of people have gathered together in beautiful baskets in order to bless me. What I don't understand is why anyone would want to place a whole fresh pineapple (but no knife) in a hotel room. What is one supposed to do with it? Now a hunk of cheese that I can bite into when I am hungry (or Godiva chocolates) is a different story. Of course, one can always get an eight-dollar coke from the mini-bar in the hotel room...but then how does one later explain the expense to the twenty-four-year-old associate pastor when he gets the bill?

MORE ON KNICKKNACKS

Now I have a few thoughts concerning all this "stuff" that begins to pile up around the house. We call these things "knickknacks"—the real meaning of which can be summed up in one sentence: "I have absolutely no

25

reason for my existence except to take up space and collect dust."

When you turn out the light and go to bed at night, are you aware of what your knickknacks are doing? Exactly! They are reproducing. An innocent calendar from Mexico soon becomes four more cloth wall calendars arriving from the four corners of the earth.

Of course you can sell these items at garage sales. Maybe someone has a void in her (or his) life for a demon-possessed wood carving of a bull or a miniature prayer tower or, perhaps, a picture (made entirely of broken shells) of Jesus praying in the garden.

Or you can save yourself some money by wrapping up your knickknack as a Christmas present and giving it to someone dear to you. The only danger is, you may run the risk of the gift making a full circle and going back to the friend who gave it to you in the first place, or even worse, it may circle right back to you!

If you get caught, you might say something like, "Well, bless the Lord, what do you think the odds are that two plastic kangaroos covered with rat hair from the Philippines exist in this city?"

Knickknacks serve absolutely no purpose except to sit on the shelf, take up space and mock you. "Dust me, dust me, dust me," is their cry.

Unfortunately, there are also a lot of knickknack Christians around. They are inexpensive, occupy space, collect dust and serve no purpose.

All right, my friend, just take a deep breath now. I know that last statement may seem harsh. You may even be saying, "That can't be God." Just hold on for a few more minutes and let me explain a little further about dishes (and knickknacks).

For a wedding gift, friends of my husband gave us

bright red and yellow Melmac dishes. The service for four included dinner plates, salad bowls, cups and saucers. The pattern was red and yellow checks with a

UNFORTUNATELY, THERE ARE ALSO A LOT OF KNICKKNACK CHRISTIANS AROUND. THEY ARE INEXPENSIVE, OCCUPY SPACE, COLLECT DUST AND SERVE NO PURPOSE.

bright green vine growing on them. I know these friends meant well, but the dishes were just plain ugly.

Even so, year after year we used those dishes. Do you know that Melmac dishes never break? Even if you decide to throw them on the floor in a fit of anger and jump up and down on them, they still won't break. They also do not melt, and certainly do not sell well in garage sales. Along with all this, Melmac dishes are never lost because they are the only dishes that will definitely be returned to you after a church function.

If you have never heard of Melmac, then you are probably under thirty. Just make a phone call to your mother and ask her; she'll remember.

37

THE NEW DISHES

My dish life was finally about to change one day when I was the guest speaker at a church conference in York, Pennsylvania. There stood a dear friend waiting to talk with me after the service.

After awhile our conversation turned to her job. She told me she worked at the local pottery factory. Stoneware had just become very popular. Do you remember stoneware? It wasn't an accident that it was called *stoneware*. It seemed as if each dinner plate weighed at least twenty-five pounds.

For a long time I had admired the "Yorktown" pattern. Unlike my old Melmac dishes, these were blue-gray with a pattern of dark blue fleur-de-lis in the center. Or you could purchase the tan and dark brown version. (The tan and brown sets were made to go with your orange, short-pile, shag carpet and those unforgettable, avocado-green, state-of-the-art appliances.)

My friend told me that she had an entire service for twelve. With her employee discount, she had only paid half price for the set at the department store where she worked. Then she had a brilliant idea! We could use her employee discount to purchase a set for me. My husband and I were newlyweds with a struggling church, so even a discounted set of dishes was out of the question for us.

The next day I visited her at her workplace, the place of many dishes. We were walking through the factory and retail store when suddenly, out of the corner of my eye, I spied a bright red sign that made the hair on my neck stand up. It read "Seconds—50 percent off!" In tiny print at the very bottom of the sign were the words, "Some items may have slight to severe flaws that might be unsuitable for human use." I eagerly asked my friend if her employee discount would also apply to "seconds."

She told me yes, but she advised that I might want to wait and save up my money to purchase the "firsts." It would require faith, prayer, patience and saving, but she assured me that it would really be better for me to wait and do it that way.

By the time she had finished giving me the warning, my shopping basket was already half-filled with those precious seconds. Doing some quick calculations in my head, I figured we could use a lot of grocery coupons, eat a lot of grocery-item samples and mooch off my mom and dad for dinner several times a week. Maybe then I could afford to get all these seconds.

Then, if I made some extra sacrifices like drinking water instead of coffee for breakfast and washing my hair and dishes with Tide (there was no such thing as a dishwasher for me), I could even swing the butter dish, serving platter, spoon rest and five-piece canister set.

Giddy with excitement, I ran through the store, adding to the growing pile. So what if I didn't have enough money left over for food. Eventually, when we could buy groceries again, I would be serving the food on beautiful matching dishes.

Visions of dinner parties and Thanksgiving Day dinners danced in my head. I would walk out of the kitchen dressed in my June Cleaver apron, carrying my lovely brown turkey to my family and five guests (I only had service for eight). It would all look quite like Norma Zimmer on the Lawrence Welk Thanksgiving Day show.

The moment I arrived home, I tore open the boxes. I carefully unwrapped and gently washed each little angel (dish, I mean) and put it in its new home, my cabinet.

The red and yellow Melmac with green ivy had mocked me once too often!

THE CRACKED POT

After I carefully stacked my dinner plates, dessert dishes and all the other pieces, I stepped back to admire my work: But wait…something was wrong. My dinner plates, which I had so carefully stacked on top of one another, now looked like the leaning tower of Pisa.

The bottoms of several plates were uneven, and the painted circle designs were not exactly circular. I shifted the plates around, thinking that would help. Maybe it would work if I put the "bad" side in the back. But no, nothing worked. No matter which way I turned those dishes, they still looked the same. *Oh well*, I told myself, *when I get them on the table, no one will know the difference.*

Then over a period of time, I began to notice small, hairline cracks in my plates. It didn't stop there though. One day my family was eating shepherd's pie—a concoction of hamburger, celery and onions covered with mashed potatoes, tiny peas and one thousand fat grams of cheese (per serving). Suddenly, I bit down on something crunchy. I thought to myself, *There isn't any crunchy ingredient in here—the celery and onions are cooked.* A few more bites and again, *crunch.* I won't bore you with the details of this next revelation, but in a word—*stoneware.*

The very thing that had been created to bless me, give me joy and remind me of God's faithfulness was now crunching in my mouth, breaking my teeth. It

30

was like eating dirt and sand. I don't know if eating a plate is harmful to your health, but it sure doesn't do anything for shepherd's pie.

One by one another plate bit the dust. During the next several years I lost an entire set of dishes, one piece at a time. The salt and pepper shakers, the

WE ARE THE CLAY, AND GOD IS THE MASTER POTTER WHO DOESN'T HAVE MUCH USE FOR KNICKKNACKS. WITH THE EXPERT TOUCH OF GOD'S HANDS UPON US, HE DETECTS AND REMOVES THE IMPURITIES AND FLAWS.

31

salad bowls...everything in that set disintegrated before my eyes (or in our mouths)!

I thought of the following verse, "Dead flies putrefy the perfumer's ointment, and cause it to give off a foul odor; so does a little folly to one respected for wisdom and honor" (Eccles. 10:1).

WE ARE THE CLAY

The owner of a pottery shop once told me that a master potter still creates his best work with his hands. With those hands, he forms a lump of clay into a lovely vase. I watched him work one day as he took a blob of wet, shapeless dough and began working it and spinning it, forming something he saw in his mind as the finished product.

BUT GOD WANTS PERFECTED VESSELS FOR HIS SERVICE.

At one point, he wrinkled up his face, totally absorbed in his work. I asked him what was wrong. He told me he could feel a small, gritty piece of undissolved sand and was trying to gently work it out. It looked just fine to me, and I told him so.

32

He said that because his work was a reflection of who *he* was, it had to be perfect before it was signed and sold.

Over and over he dipped his hands in the bowl of water that sat next to him. The water was used to keep his hands wet, because it was essential for him to make sure the clay did not get dry. As long as he kept wetting it, he could work with it. If it became dry, it would harden prematurely and be susceptible to breakage. If this happened, it would end up in the scrap box.

This is a wonderful description of the way God deals with us in our lives. God led the prophet Jeremiah to the potter's house where he saw a live demonstration of God's process for making and molding His servants.

We are the clay, and God is the Master Potter who doesn't have much use for knickknacks. The water is the Holy Spirit, which must be applied liberally to keep us pliable. With the expert touch of God's hands upon us, He detects and removes the impurities and flaws that would otherwise yield weaknesses in us when heat, pressure and stress are applied, weaknesses that would render us useless and remove God's anointing from our lives.

Even Samson didn't realize when the anointing had lifted from him. That's why at first glance we appear great. We seem fine. We have no clue as to why God would have to work on us.

But God wants perfected vessels for His service. You can use a shard, a broken piece of pottery, to offer someone a drop or two of water. But a large, perfected vessel has the capacity for being used to pour out a long, cool drink to a dry, thirsty soul.

Stay on the Potter's wheel. Never cry out, "That's it, I'm done. I'm out of here." Don't let your pride, arrogance or fear cause you to hop off the Potter's wheel.

Knickknack or a vessel of honor—it's your choice!

33

CHAPTER 4

GUILT-FREE
DAYS

can't say that I was totally comfortable with
it. This is because having three sets of little
hands brushing my hair—or should I say
pulling my hair out of my head—left little
room for comfort.

Lydia had arranged a bright pink bow on the top of
my head. Abagael strategically placed an orange and
yellow squeezee so that it appeared as if I had sticks of
weeds growing out of my ear.

Hadassah's pudgy little two-year-old fingers couldn't
manage the assorted clips and bows lying all over my
bed, so she just wrapped the round bristle brush through
strands of hair until the brush was permanently stuck in
the new nest.

Pleased with their creation, they unanimously
decided that now I needed makeup applied. Of course,
the only available stuff around was my treasured,
expensive, Bobbie Brown brand, which had been a precious gift to me.

I really needed to get out of bed and put on my
clothes. I needed to make the bed. There were dishes
to wash, e-mails to answer and the way, way past due
book deadline.

Instead of listening to the sounds from mounds of
duties beckoning to me, I sank a little deeper in the bed
covers and let my three little girls give me a makeover.

"Done," they exclaimed triumphantly. They knew
they were done because all the makeup was gone.
"Mommy pretty," chirped my baby. They had poked
at my eyes with mascara wands, applied three different
colors of blush and used half a bottle of liquid foundation to complete the look, covering my face with a
perfectly circular mask.

When my oldest daughter entered the room, she

stood there in disbelief and gasped, "Oh my!" Hadassah announced to her sister, "Mommy pretty," as Jerusha let me know I was the most hysterically funny-looking model she had ever seen. "Are you going for the clown look?" she asked. Then doubling over with laughter, she called out as she left the room, "You forgot Mommy's accessories."

At that suggestion, my three little makeup artists made a beeline for my drawers and pulled out jewelry and scarves. In a few moments I was really decked out. But the girls weren't finished yet. "Wait a minute!" yelled five-year-old Abagael as she ran down the hall toward her bedroom. She returned, proudly carrying a plastic tiara, which she promptly imbedded into my skull.

This wasn't Saturday. On Saturday you can mess around with your kids for an hour. This was a week day. Week days are made for work. Responsible people do not play beauty shop on their beds for two hours during the morning of a work day.

I could not believe how incredibly guilty I felt sitting there, laughing and playing with my children, wasting valuable time that could be used to clean my silverware drawer (you know, the place where food droppings gather). I could also be reading my Bible, watching TBN or planting an organic garden. OK, not actually planting a garden, but maybe at least cleaning out my vegetable drawer in the refrigerator. Instead, my little girls were inexplicably delighted with their human mannequin.

37

STOP AND ENJOY

Stop and think of the times when we shove out of the

way the very ones we are working so hard for. Little children have a very short attention span. It wasn't long before mine left their mannequin and scampered off to watch their brothers dismantle the dining room to make a tent.

Before Lydia left my room, she called back over her shoulder, "Don't take anything off, Mommy. You are beautiful." It was as if she read my mind. My hand was already on my cheeks to remove the imbedded, decorative blush.

All morning I was met with snickers and some really rude comments from other members of my household. Actually, I thought I looked better than some Paris runway models. I wonder if my two-year-old moonlights as a stylist for those fashion shows?

Just like you, I have heard some of the greatest preaching and teaching. As it comes from the pulpit it is meant to get us to rise up, press on, possess the victory, take hold of our healing, claim prosperity and such. There is great truth in all of it. In fact, I have often preached some of it myself.

Often the emphasis is to do more, give more, attend more and work more continually. As a result we can end up feeling guilty about any time we spend not directly associated with achieving more, crossing lines and going higher.

I made an amazing discovery that day I spent time playing "Dress Up Mommy" with my girls, even though my calendar was filled up until the millennium and we had a very busy ministry touching people all over the world for Jesus. Our home is a lively mix of squeals of joy and a flurry of commands to get to the dinner table, pick up your clothes, hurry and get in the car or we're going to be late for school or church again. There is shoes-shopping, dance classes, karate and swim team practices. Life is full, busy and even blessed.

I THINK JESUS WAS A REALLY SMART MAN WHO UNDERSTOOD THE NEED FOR REST, FELLOWSHIP (EATING) AND EVEN ENJOYMENT.

But I was horribly unhappy. I never seemed to finish anything. Guilt was my constant companion. Joy was sporadic. The more I looked around at the mess, the more frustrated I became.

39

Sound familiar? Are you overwhelmed? I know there are some women out there who have immaculate homes, dust-free baseboards and no clothes waiting in the hamper to be washed. Christmas shopping is finished in August, and they actually have kept up with their one-year Bible studies. That, my disappointed friend, is not me!

Jesus always had the work of the ministry to do. People were always following Him around for "a word." But I can just see Him relaxing with Mary, Martha and Lazarus at their home.

He was probably lying on the floor, resting His head

on some really soft pillows. Do you think He felt guilty as He popped one of Martha's city-wide-famous appetizers in His mouth? No, I think Jesus was a really smart man who understood the need for rest, fellowship (eating) and even enjoyment.

DOES YOUR HOUSE REALLY NEED TO BE SPOTLESS?

Because I travel on the weekends, I have to move into the "Mom, ruler of the universe" mode during the week—shouting commands of "Pick up your sneakers," "Where's your homework?" "Don't bug your brother," "Let's go, let's go, let's go." Often I sound like a really annoying Marine drill sergeant. Is it any wonder the children roll their eyes at me? After all, I am doing this for their good!

Who in the world would want to live with that 24/7?

I know, I *really* know that Jesus is coming, and we must reinforce our positive image thinking in order to possess and overcome.

But we also need to be nice. We need to hang around church just a little longer to speak to that newly saved single mom who needs encouragement.

We also need to watch cartoons with our kids, take the time to swim with them, bike with them and even color with them. All this must be done without screaming—even when they are getting green and yellow crayons on your new table.

My parents were two of the most wonderful people on earth. My mother is a saint!—Saint Rose, the all-patient one. She raised three kids, worked a forty-hour work week and worked by my dad's side when he decided to pioneer a church that involved having

40

services in her house. She played the piano for church, sang solos, taught Sunday school and children's church and, lest we forget this one, cleaned the church when the assigned person didn't show up (which was often).

She also made most of my clothes because Daddy's small salary couldn't keep me in style and she didn't want me to look different from the other girls. I remember the time she bribed me by promising to make me a pantsuit if I would go to a ladies' banquet and play the piano for her while she sang. I know I should have done it willingly, but hey, a new outfit is a new outfit—any way you can get it!

All this was before fast food, so every Thursday night after work she shopped for groceries at Weiss Grocery Store in Hanover, Pennsylvania (they gave double green stamps there). She always budgeted enough money for us to eat out at the Victory Restaurant after she finished shopping. I can still see my dad looking at the bill and shaking his head as he said, "Five dollars! Five dollars just to take a family of five out for dinner!" This was heavy stuff in 1968.

41

Saturday was what I called "Cleaning Day From Hell." Mom was always up at 7 A.M. (a totally ungodly hour) barking orders while Mr. Clean, Clorox and the brand-new discovery Mop-n-Glo went room to room with her.

My brothers didn't do diddly-squat! They went out to play, because boys didn't clean back then. Once I locked the door to my room, put on my Monkees album and, using my blue hair brush for a microphone, practiced my Nancy Sinatra, Jr. moves in front of the mirror. I was supposed to be changing all the bed sheets, but how could I help it? I just didn't feel like changing sheets.

After about two hours, my mom became suspicious and broke through the door, hands on hips, eyes

MY SEVEN-YEAR-OLD HAS A BARBIE COMPUTER WITH FIFTY DISCS, A TV AND AN OLD STEREO. BUT WHAT SHE REALLY WANTS IS ME!

burning holes through my head just as I was finishing "Daydream Believer." I don't really remember much more of that day. Someone told me that you tend to block out really horrible memories.

42

Now please, don't think my mom is a shrew. She is the sweetest, hardest-working person I know, even to this day. Maybe the women of her generation had better genes than we do. Or could it be the diet pills?

MAKING WHAT
REALLY COUNTS COUNT

My parents spent so much of their lives working... working in the ministry, working at full-time and part-time jobs and raising three children, all with a minimum amount of money. But they did it. And what do we remember?

We remember the grocery shopping trips and the

"Can-we-really-afford-it?" five-dollar dinners at the Victory Restaurant. And I might add, we remember those horrible camping trips we took because my dad desperately wanted us to have a family vacation but that was all we could afford.

Today, my kids go to McDonalds, Burger King and Toys-backward-R-the-Lechners regularly. Even I am sick of hearing myself say, "You kids don't appreciate anything. My mom had to walk five miles in the snow, uphill, just to buy me a Happy Meal."

My seven-year-old has a Barbie computer with fifty discs, a TV and an old stereo. She even saved up her Christmas and birthday monies and bought herself a "sound machine," so she can now sleep to the sounds of sea gulls and ocean noises.

But what she really wants is me! She wants a not-so-stressed-out mom who will watch a Veggie Tales video, curled up with her in her bed with popcorn.

If you are like me, you fall into bed with a hundred things left undone. I don't have a to-do list because then I would actually have to sit down and write one out. That would really make me feel guilty, because my children would find it after I died at the age of 109. They would then laugh hysterically because they would realize that I had only fulfilled the first item on the list:

1. Make a to-do list

You may be hopelessly or mildly unorganized. Please don't stop working on that based on my testimony. You cannot reclaim yesterday. You only have today.

We have unrealistic goals based on our faulty belief that everyone else has their lives completely together.

As I look out my front window at all of the lovely homes that line our block, I feel absolutely sure that

43

they have no juice stains on their "no-stain-forever" carpets. And surely no three-year-old French fries stick under the driver's seat of their minivans.

"LORD, HERE IS YOUR SERVANT CATHY SHOWING UP FOR DUTY. WHAT DO YOU DESIRE FOR ME TO DO TODAY?"

The enemy will work overtime to deliver an imagination to you to try to make you feel guilty, worthless and miserable. He wants you to feel just like a failure.

Life isn't perfect; only Jesus is perfect. It's OK to lower your expectations about having an immaculate house. Two of our children are severely dyslexic. They attend a highly demanding, highly academically rated school where they struggle for a "C."

To counteract feeling like a bad mother whose child is destined to work at a snail-tasting factory, I changed my expectation. I no longer expect perfection—from me or anyone else. This is what stopped me from driving myself crazy. More importantly, I *encourage* my children rather than *drive* them.

Lowering expectations is not the same as rising up in faith. In fact, your faith can score highly in areas that are really important, while rug spots, toilet mildew and three missed spelling words no longer rock your world.

Feeling better yet?

BE MOTIVATED BY HIS LOVE

I have a simple, little spiritual exercise that I do every morning (when I can remember to do it and don't have cramps).

As soon as my eyes open, unless of course there is a four-year-old putting Sugar Pops up my nose, I say, "Lord, here is Your servant Cathy showing up for duty. What do You desire for me to do today?"

Your first thought might be, *He wants me to pray for four hours and fast for ten days.* Well, you know good and well that was not God. So you just wait. He will speak to you. His Word says that you are His sheep and you hear His voice. He won't ask you to do more than you are able. He will ask you to obey Him and to respond in faith.

God doesn't use disappointment and guilt to try to motivate us. He encourages us through His goodness and mercy and by showing us the results of faith and obedience.

I hate to think how low His expectations of me have been at times.

45

Just as good parents desire their child to succeed, so your Father desires for you to succeed.

My son has to work so incredibly hard to learn his letters. It comes naturally to his brother, and that is frustrating for him.

But he takes his clues from me. As I am kind and loving, firm but patient, it helps my child to relax and learn. And that is what Jesus does...He helps us.

We are not hopeless without Him—only helpless.

Now get up and clean those baseboards!

CHAPTER 5

STOP HITTING ME IN THE HEAD WITH YOUR BANNER, PLEASE

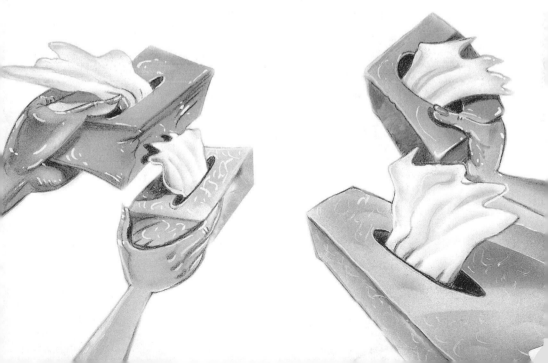

or the life of me, I simply cannot understand how the words on that paper go through a little black machine and, with the speed of light, appear in a machine at my mom's house.

Where do those words go? Through a little cord and up over the house like a television signal?

Those profound thoughts ran through my mind as I finished writing by hand chapter four of this book and faxed it over to my mom, Saint Rose (see chapter four). She, in turn, will try to decipher my scribbling, type, edit and then send it on to my longsuffering editor.

By the way, I typed this chapter on my husband's laptop computer. Mom will be so proud of me when it comes through her little machine.

People like me are totally clueless and have been hopelessly left behind in the electronic super highway. I am more in the '73 Chevy Impala technology.

The same principle applies to faith, healing and miracles. My mind can't wrap itself around the concepts, and yet, without understanding, I have seen them work.

48

Do you ever feel lazy because God just interrupted your life with an absolutely amazing miracle when you were not standing, confessing and believing? Actually, the miracle was simply the goodness of God to you.

Faith is really simple. It is a trust and a belief that God will actually do what He said He would do.

I CAN'T BELIEVE THIS IS HAPPENING

We were in the middle of frenzied worship when a dear sweet saint (who I am sure meant well) ran to the front of the auditorium to grab a "Jesus the King" banner.

Now the first problem was that the banner was about ten feet high, made with about fifty pounds of wood for the pole and one hundred yards of white and purple satin embroidered with gold fabric for the banner.

The second problem was that she actually thought God had told her to run up, get the banner and pass it over all our heads.

FAITH IS REALLY SIMPLE. IT IS A TRUST AND A BELIEF THAT GOD WILL ACTUALLY DO WHAT HE SAID HE WOULD DO.

My eyes were closed, and my hands were raised in worship, but this was just too much. I kept my hands up. After all, I was the guest speaker and had to set the example, but I slowly opened both eyes to see the drama that was unfolding.

49

She was only about four-feet, ten-inches tall, so she staggered backward as she lifted the banner out of its stand. Two people started to make a move to help her, but they backed away thinking they would be quenching the Spirit.

My immediate thought was, *Please take the chance of quenching the Spirit before she decapitates the worship team.*

From this point on, everything went totally south. After she managed to get to the back of the auditorium with the "killer banner," she proceeded up the middle aisle waving the huge banner back and forth as "the Spirit led her."

She was hitting the first four people on each side of her, row by row. It frightened an elderly lady who

IN ORDER TO LIVE IN THIS WORLD, WITH ALL THE PRESSURES, WE NEED THE FULLNESS OF JOY.

didn't see her coming. The white, gold and purple mass of cloth fell on the woman's head while she was either in deep meditation or asleep.

Up the aisle the woman with the banner continued to come, swinging, swaying and hitting. The minister of music stood on the platform appalled, his mouth hung open in disbelief.

I propose a new church ordinance. No one under five-feet, six-inches tall can legally carry a banner. And while we are on the subject, I also propose that no one who can't clap in time to the music should have a tambourine. AND dancers must, at all times, keep those sticks with the long, wavy, ribbon thingies out of my hair.

This is just my personal opinion, of course. I'm sure I'll receive letters from dear saints who are being led by the Spirit. Also, ladies, if you must order your dance out-fit in size XXXL, you might want to dance in the back of the sanctuary or alongside of the church pews. Not out-side the church, just behind or alongside the pews.

I used to weigh 265 pounds, so I do not discriminate against overweight people in any way. I was just sure that no one in their right mind, no matter how Christian they are, would enjoy seeing me leaping around the stage wearing a white leotard with a gold cummerbund and a Star of David on my head. No, no! That is not a blessing. Better keep that in my private time so only God can appreciate it.

BACK TO FAITH

Sorry for the rabbit trail...now back to faith. I cannot separate faith from hope, nor hope from love. For me, faith and hope and love must come hand in hand with joy—inexplicable, uproarious, phenomenal, belly-tickling, laugh-out-loud JOY.

People get drunk and laugh really loud. They also throw up a lot. People do drugs and laugh, but they also see pink elephants and die. But I don't know of anyone who got gloriously, wonderfully and remarkably filled to overflowing with faith, hope, love and joy who then threw up or died.

Oh, how I love the presence of the Lord, for in His presence is fullness of joy. In order to live in this world, with all the pressures, we need the fullness of joy. I don't know if I have ever been full, totally full to the top with no room for more!

Because events are fleeting, joy doesn't just ride on happy happenings. Joy comes from what God means to you—in spite of your circumstances. Once you get to that point, no one can take it away from you.

LAUGHTER CAN COME IN UNEXPECTED WAYS

Miami...the year was 1988, or 1985, or, oh well, who

51

cares what year it was. I was the scheduled speaker for a Woman's Aglow monthly meeting. The crown on my front tooth had come loose and fallen off while I was brushing my teeth—the last task I had to do before they came for me at my hotel.

My ride would be here in minutes, and I was scrambling to find some Super Glue. When I finally found

WHEN YOU WANT TO CRY...LAUGH— RESPONSIBLE PEOPLE LAUGH!

it, the top was glued shut to the tube. I couldn't find a pin to make another hole, so I frantically tried chewing off the glue from the top of the tube.

52

After squirting some into my mouth, I applied some of it to the crown of my tooth and glued it back into place. I held it tightly in place for the required twenty seconds. Suddenly, I discovered that I could not pull my finger loose. My finger was actually glued to my tooth! I felt like Lucy Ricardo in a sitcom. My ride pulled up and beeped and beeped. Panic time! This was not something I could cover up with a broach or a scarf. I just sat on the end of the bed and began to laugh. What a sight!

I thought, *I bet Gloria Copeland or Marilyn Hickey never had these problems.* And I laughed some more. My ride decided to come and see what was holding me up. More laughter. Miraculously, she had a little bottle of nail polish remover and carefully dumped a couple ounces into my mouth. Finger free and tooth in place, we left for the meeting. I was in great shape, except that for some strange reason my mouth tasted like an old, dirty sock.

The irony of it all was that the subject of my message that morning was "Having Joy in Difficult Situations." Talk about an illustrated sermon!

When you want to cry…laugh. If you must start out crying, end up laughing. RESPONSIBLE PEOPLE LAUGH!

DIFFERENT DEGREES OF JOY!

Joy, like sorrow, pain, grief, happiness and *shalom* (peace) come in different degrees.

I did not realize until much later in life that I had been struggling as a young woman as a manic-depressive person. That image conjures up people who look like axe murderers, but in reality, it is just a term for someone who has very high highs and very low lows—and not much room in the middle.

Depression is a horrible thing. It ranges from just feeling a little low to being suicidal. Based upon my own experience in ministering to people, I would say that depression is on the rise.

I have friends who are always on the mountaintop or somewhere near there. If they are not experiencing a deep revelation and the glory twenty-four hours a day, seven days a week, they think something is drastically wrong. If you are not floating around on the glory cloud with them, they think there is something drastically wrong with you.

Joy is not measured by how often we shout, "Oh hallelujah, I'm so excited." That's a good place to be, but I can also just be in my kitchen cooking a meatloaf

53

and feel an overwhelming sense of the presence of God. I feel His mercy and wonderful joy all around me.

One of the best pictures ever taken of my brothers and me was snapped an hour after we buried our father. Believe me, I am not photogenic. This started right after I was born and continued throughout my whole life—even Glamour Shots couldn't perform their usual

SOMETIMES 90 PERCENT OF YOUR BATTLE IS IN JUST ENDURING TO THE END.

miracle. What a disappointment. But on this day, at this particular time, I looked kinda pretty. My hair actually cooperated, my makeup was good (even after crying for hours), and I didn't look enormous!

54

When I was so totally dependent on my heavenly Father to get me through those tough days, Jesus had just pushed through and shone through me.

That picture sits on a shelf in my family room as a reminder of what God can do. Everyone who sees the picture remarks about how pretty I look. They ask me why. I tell them it is because at one of the lowest points in my life, the Holy Spirit simply overshadowed me.

I am reminded of little Mary who simply couldn't comprehend why an angel (who probably scared her head covering off) would come to her with the information that she was going to bear the Son of God. After several desperate protests and questions, she could only say, "Let it be to me according to your word" (Luke 1:38).

Even in her utter disbelief, the true weight of what she was about to undergo must have caused her to walk around in a daze. The Holy Spirit overshadowed her. He does the same for you. Even after your personal ordeal is over, you may have absolutely no idea how you ever got through your crisis.

I'll tell you what happened, darling. The Holy Spirit overshadowed you. In my case, He made me somewhat attractive. ONLY GOD CAN DO THAT.

My second book was titled *Couldn't We Just Kill 'em and Tell God They Died?* We had some extremely mixed opinions about that title. Someone even suggested that the word "kill" and "God" could not possibly work together in a title. They obviously have never read the Bible.

I talked to a pastor friend, Michael Thorne, after one morning service. He's a great guy and one of only five people who can really make me laugh. Like most of us, he's really had a rough year.

Walking me out to the parking lot he said, "Cathy I'm going to write a book and call it *God, You Can Just Kill Me, Because I Can't Go Through This Any More.*" I thought it was a funny title, one that many of us can associate with.

A faith statement that may not be very encouraging but is full of truth is this: Sometimes 90 percent of your battle is in just enduring to the end. (Sounds like the old testimonies we used to hear in prayer meeting.)

Giving up would actually be easier. Dying would sometimes be less painful. Living and breathing, when the weight of heartache, pain, loneliness, sorrow, grief and regret are present, can be almost unbearably hard.

Go Ahead and Jump

A few weeks ago my cell phone rang, and I actually answered it. Most of my friends and family will tell you that this was in itself just short of miraculous.

On the other end was a friend of mine, who began

THE ENEMY WAVES HIS BANNER IN YOUR FACE, TRYING TO DEMAND THAT YOU LISTEN.

speaking abruptly in tense, desperate sentences.

"Cathy, I'm standing at the top of the Howard Franklin Bridge. Give me one reason why I should not jump."

Now this is a guy who is always joking around, and I had no reason to believe this time was any different.

"Oh, you silly man, what are you doing?"

"Cathy, I'm dead serious. Tell me one thing that will stop me from jumping."

He was apparently using his cell phone, because I could hear the sound of car horns beeping and people occasionally yelling things I could not decipher.

I thought this had to be an elaborate setup. So realistic. Dave would do anything for a laugh.

I began to think about the struggle he has had with his marriage and kids, and I remember thinking, *Go ahead, Dave, jump. I think I would, too.*

But I told him, "Dave, man, this is NOT funny." Now I was pacing around my bedroom, cell phone in hand, visualizing my friend dangling between heaven and earth. I thought, *If he jumps and they find his phone, my number will be the last number recorded. They'll all think I counseled him to jump.*

"Twenty-four hours, Dave."

"What?"

"In twenty-four hours God could turn your entire situation around, but you'll never know it if you don't hold on."

I could feel his mind and heart desperately trying to grasp a truth, something to give him hope.

Miraculously, I heard a heavy sigh and then soft weeping. The car door opened, then a ding-ding and then the slam.

"Okay, Cath. I'm going home. I'll call you in the morning." Click. I could scarcely breath. I could not move. What had just happened?

The enemy lost. That's what happened. You know his job is to get you to believe all hope is gone…nothing will ever change…the cancer has won…the divorce is final…the ministry is over. He does his job very well. I hate him all the more for that.

My job is to stand in the earth, waving a flag (not literally) and declaring God's character to all those who will listen.

The enemy waves his banner in your face, trying to demand that you listen. He assaults your senses, distracts your perception and twists God's words just to make you ever so slightly begin to doubt them.

I'm like the banner lady, waving my banner, hitting you in the head just to get your attention.

"Twenty-four hours, my friend. Twenty-four hours and God can turn this entire situation around." I am being led by the Spirit to hit you!

Now, get in your car and go home and call me in the morning.

57

CHAPTER 6

IF YOU DON'T LIKE IT, DON'T BLAME GOD

Have you ever heard anyone say, "I'm going to walk with Jesus, I'm going to love God and I'm going to serve God. But then ten years from now, I'm going to backslide. I'm going to commit adultery, I'm going to mess up my life, I'm going to ruin my kids' lives, and I'm going to destroy the church. Then I'll repent, write another book and appear on TBN."

If we asked any great man of God like Jim Bakker or Jimmy Swaggart or others who have seen God's grace, I am sure any one of them would say that he would not have chosen the same path—even though he has won a lot of people in jail to Christ or now has a ministry to drug addicts. I'm certain each one of them would say they would not take the same path again.

I'm sure no one starts out their life in Christ by saying, "Ten years from now I'm going to ruin my life and mess everybody else up." Instead, we are all like Peter who said he would never fail the Lord, never walk away, never sin. Yes, we do need to have an attitude that says, "I'll always follow You, Lord." But we also have to recognize that "the heart is deceitful above all things, and desperately wicked; who can know it?" (Jer. 17:9).

What happens in the lives of men or women that causes them suddenly to walk out of the grace, the anointing, the call or the blessing of God? It actually does not happen suddenly at all. It doesn't happen overnight. It's something that takes place over a period of time if you are not guarding and watching diligently over your heart, if you are not casting down vain imaginations or if you are not in the Word. How does this actually happen in someone's life? It happens way back when with that first evil thought, that first word, that first temptation. When it was not cast down right away, it began to build.

WALKING OUT OF THE GRACE OF GOD HAPPENS WITH THAT FIRST EVIL THOUGHT, WORD OR TEMPTATION.

Pondering this reminds me of the time I shared the speakers' platform with a dear person. I couldn't help but notice that she kept her distance from me. She and her husband were well-known pastors of one of the largest churches in the world. They had been married the same length of time as my husband and me. It came as a surprise to me when I later heard that she had divorced her husband. She told people that she didn't want her life the way it was anymore. What happened?

61

DISCONTENTMENT IS DANGEROUS BUSINESS

She didn't just wake up one morning while she was loving on and serving Jesus and say, "I don't want to be married anymore." Something happened long before that. I don't know what the Lord has shown others, but as I prayed, the Lord showed me that this kind of change begins with discontentment—just plain discontentment. I'm not talking here about praying and believing for God to change a particular situation. I am talking about the kind of discontentment that involves losing the joy and the wonder of childlike faith. That's when we begin to be discontented with what we have.

We then start looking at what we have and begin assessing that we don't like any of it. You attend many churches, but none of them really bless you. You don't know what's going on in your marriage. Some may call it a midlife crisis or something else, but it's really plain old discontentment. There is a scripture that says, "Because you did not serve the LORD your God with joy and gladness of heart, for the abundance of everything, therefore you shall serve your enemies, whom the LORD will send against you" (Deut. 28:47–48). What one thing offended God the most about the children of Israel? I believe He was most offended by their discontent with everything.

If you're in a conversation with a discontented person, it doesn't take you long to find out who that person is upset with or mad at. Very quickly you find out why he or she doesn't attend a certain church anymore, and on and on. There is no joy in that person's life. Often that person doesn't even realize it all started out with discontent.

Many people are discontented in their marriages. "How much longer am I going to have to put up with this guy?" "How am I going to deal with this marriage?" "I don't know how much longer I can put up with this situation."

DON'T SING "ACHY, BREAKY HEART"

Anyone can fall prey to discontent. I have had to

watch over my own heart concerning my house. We came home from a few days' vacation to find half of our home saturated with water. The water heater in the attic above our bedroom had burst while we were away. Since no one was home to see the water trickling down the walls and turn it off, the water kept running until the bathroom floor could no longer

SOME MAY CALL IT A MIDLIFE CRISIS OR SOMETHING ELSE, BUT IT'S REALLY PLAIN OLD DISCONTENTMENT.

hold the weight and the ceiling under it fell down, allowing the water to run freely, soaking everything in its path—furniture, clothing and all the carpeting.

63

As I lay on the couch looking at my surroundings, I thought, *It looks like we are camping!* My husband, Randi, was asleep in the recliner, and Jerusha our daughter slept on another couch. I thought, *Why would anyone in his right mind put a water heater in the attic to begin with? And of all weeks to burst—the week we were gone.*

There is a song about an achy, breaky heart. Well, I was waking up every morning with achy, breaky bones! It was easy to cry out to God to tell Him that I wanted my bed back. I felt like shouting, "Hey, God, I can't live like this any longer!"

If you are not careful, bitterness will spill out of your mouth. The mouth is so important. We need to be filled with the Spirit of God every day. Do you know why? It's because our mouths leak.

Discontentment will open up many unwanted doors. You may not like your situation. In fact, as you read this you may be in a situation you know God doesn't want you in. You know He is going to change it, but you're not there yet.

We all have been there. Everyone's problem is different. Some situations are worse than others. Some circumstances are hard to understand.

For example, I was once discussing with someone the passing of a dear friend, Ellen. During our conversation this woman expressed how she couldn't understand why Ellen had died because she had prophecies that hadn't been fulfilled before her death. She said, "Cathy, you always said that nothing can happen to you until your prophecies are fulfilled." I told her that we are always going to live with unfulfilled words.

This reminds me of how Moses kept going until God said it was time. The Israelites were a nation of discontented people. I imagine he had enough and said, "Look, I'm going to heaven to get away from you people."

People get discontented over the slightest things. My children can be watching television when one of those weather-warning signals comes across the screen and disrupts the program they are engrossed in. They are ready to throw something at the TV because they have no patience. You can understand that with little children, but it is not acceptable behavior for adults.

Which button does the enemy have to push in you to make you discontented and upset? One of the hardest things to learn to do is (one of my favorite sayings), "Just spit and go on." Can you say, "OK, this stinks. I don't like it, and I don't know how to change it, but I'm not going to let this situation keep me from the blessing God has for me. I will not allow it to take my joy today."

WE NEED TO BE FILLED WITH THE SPIRIT OF GOD EVERY DAY— BECAUSE OUR MOUTHS LEAK.

I remember hearing Larry Lea teach on forgiveness. He said, "Don't nurse it, curse it or rehearse it." The more people you tell about a situation you are facing, the deeper that root of bitterness gets in you.

Do you know that you can be *faithful* without being *loyal?* This can happen in your marriage, even though you wouldn't dream of going out and committing adultery. I know men and women who are faithful, but they are not loyal. Loyalty makes the difference. Joseph discovered that in Potiphar's house.

65

> Thus he left all that he had in Joseph's hand, and he did not know what he had except for the bread which he ate. Now Joseph was handsome in form and appearance.
>
> —GENESIS 39:6

Joseph was handpicked by God to excel and to be promoted. We have often heard it said that the way up is first down. Every person whom God elevates, uses and honors must first go down before he goes up.

WHAT GOES UP MUST FIRST COME DOWN

We live in a country, unfortunately, where almost everything is based on the bottom line—"What's in it for me?" Even the prophetic ministry has spoiled people. People will come to meetings just to get a prophecy, and if they don't get one, they get mad.

I was in a meeting in Orlando when a lady approached me and said, "I want my check back or I'll stop payment on it, and we'll see how you feel about that." She was angry because she didn't get a personal prophecy. I thought to myself, *And that's exactly why you didn't get a word.* I have heard Bishop Hamon often say that he has seen people hang around a meeting waiting for a personal prophecy. Then when God tells him to stop the meeting, some of those same people grab their Bibles and stomp out of the church—mad. God wanted to reveal to them what was in their hearts more then He wanted them to receive a word from the Lord.

Yes, we must remember that God has no trouble speaking to us at any time. But we must also remember that the heart is deceitfully wicked. So much so that we may even judge the actions of others and say we would never be capable of doing the things they do. However, we must remember that it is by faith we wouldn't do those things. That this is why we need the Holy Spirit so much.

HE SHAPES OUR CHARACTER

Joseph got all these prophetic dreams. He ran and told his brothers about them, about how they were all bowing down to him. Even before that, his brothers had hated him anyway because he was Daddy's favorite. Their father had many children, but Benjamin and

Joseph, the children by his beloved wife, Rachel, were his favorites. Remember, he had to marry Leah first in order to marry Rachel. Can you imagine the spirit of rejection that Leah must have had? "I have to marry this man who does not love me and does not want me."

It reminds me of when Prince Charles and Princess Di got married. Some media people reported that it was an arranged marriage, but the whole world thought it was a beautiful storybook romance. Actually, according to a biographer, Diana had been chosen as a suitable wife. But she was also in love with Charles (or with the idea of being in love). However, Charles, who was thirty years old, reportedly said, "I hate to do this." He was reportedly told, "Charles, just close your eyes and think of England." How sad.

Joseph's brothers were angry because they knew he was favored. They wanted their dad's affection them-selves. Of course, Joseph was not only chosen by his father—he was also chosen by God. He was probably a spoiled brat. Didn't his dad make him a special coat? He didn't just want to *buy* him something nice—he *made* a coat for him. This was an act of covenant, because part of the covenant was an exchanging of the coat. When his dad made that coat, basically he was saying, "I am bypassing the oldest brother, changing the rules and you are going to be the one to inherit my blessing." Exchanging the coat made the brothers angrier, because they knew it should have been made for Reuben, the oldest son.

67

This gift gave the impression that Joseph was going to succeed his father. It would be like today's British royal family bypassing Prince William, who is in line to be king, and choosing a child born to the king's true love.

TONGUE CONTROL

Joseph, who was young and undoubtedly spoiled, blabbed his dream to his brothers. One of the first signs of immaturity is a lack of tongue control. That's why children say everything that pops into their heads, and you want to strangle them.

GOD GIVES US WHAT WE CAN HANDLE AT ONE TIME.

I so admire Darlene from Hillsong. She is so thin, and rightly so. She bounces continually during her singing and burns all those calories. When my seven-year-old daughter heard me make a comment about how beautiful and thin Darlene is, she went directly to Darlene, whom she just adores, and said, "My mother says you're bony."

I wanted to crawl in a hole, but I told Darlene, "In America, that's really a good thing."

Children have no discernment about when to keep their mouths shut. I always tell my children, "Those things you hear are Lechner things. Don't repeat them." Gabriel is great at telling it all. He hugs everyone, including the UPS man. We really do believe he is going to be a pastor.

In Scripture we can see that Joseph had no tongue control. First, he told his brothers the first dream. Then when he had another dream, what did he do? That's right; he blabbed it even though he knew how mad his brothers were about the first one.

We have always felt sorry for Joseph and the predicaments he got in. But we need to realize that God sent him to Egypt. Yes, we see the big picture of how God used him to provide for his whole family in the end. However, the bigger picture was that Joseph had some serious character problems.

GOD WILL ONLY GIVE YOU WHAT YOU CAN HANDLE

God wants to give you everything you want, plus things you never ask for. You want to get married? God wants that for you, too. You want children? God wants them for you. You want a ministry? God wants to give it to you. It's not a matter of God withholding things from you. You have to be found faithful when these things come to you. If I gave my five-year-old the car keys and told her to drive herself to school, she'd do severe damage even before she got out of the driveway, simply because she can't handle a car.

God gives us what we can handle at one time. You have a choice. You can go around the mountain again, or you can learn your lesson, suck it up, stop feeling sorry for yourself and press forward.

If the Lord tarries, I'm going to be raising six teenagers all at the same time. Along with Jerusha, who is now in her twenties, I also have three children who are seven years old, one who is five, one four and one who is two. I'm not waiting until they are teenagers before I begin to prepare them. I have to take the time to do that now. The Lord wants us to invest ourselves in our children now so that down the line, we won't have smart-aleck teenagers we are ashamed to take

69

anywhere. We don't want to come up in the prayer line asking for prayer for a teen who has pierced himself shut.

I took Jerusha all over the world with me. She never back-talked me or brought shame on the character of Jesus, and she loves going to church. If you do your job right, you can raise children who love God. If you began this too late, it's OK, because God will cause crop failure to your old crop. He'll curse that old crop and cause good crop to come in instead. If you have grown children, your children will come in. He's made a covenant that includes your kids.

THE PIT WHERE THERE IS NO WATER

Joseph's brothers saw Joseph with that coat of many colors. They couldn't stand the sight of him because they were so filled with anger and hate. They laid their plans to get rid of him. However, Reuben, their older brother, said, "We can't go through with this. It will break our father's heart. I don't like him any more than you do, but there's got to be another way" (paraphrased). (See Genesis 37.) So they put him in a pit where there was no water.

Let me tell you this: If God has His hand on you to raise you up for service to Him, you may have to go to a pit where there is no water. You may be in a situation where those who see you will wonder what you did to cause God to put you in such a horrible place. They will ask, "If God is really with you, why are you in this situation?" You will even go through things that will cause others to believe that God has surely forsaken you.

You may begin to question God: "Don't you know my rent is due?" or " My biological clock is ticking away." The phrase "It's not fair" is a familiar phrase—one we repeat over and over. Don't you know that the dealings of God don't always seem fair to us? They are not going to be like the world. You can either fall on the rock, or the rock will fall on you.

IF GOD HAS HIS HAND ON YOU TO RAISE YOU UP FOR SERVICE TO HIM, YOU MAY HAVE TO GO TO A PIT WHERE THERE IS NO WATER.

Joseph was sold into slavery. His brothers took the coat that represented his inheritance. It represented all those dreams that he had. It represented the promise of God. He was stripped of his promise. Like Joseph, if God has His hand on you for anything, you will go through a place where it seems as though your vision has died—not just once, but many times over again. It will look like the very thing God told you He was going to do, He changed His mind about and is not going to do it now.

You may begin to cry and be ready to give up. You may decide not to walk with God anymore. Let me tell you, feeling like that is a good sign. Why? Because it's a sign you are in boot camp, and God is training you.

Let me advise you not to be so quick to judge someone who is going through a hard place. We are always ready to offer advice to others. "Are you reading your Bible? Are you studying, praying, fasting?" It may just be that they are in the pit of God's dealing. It's not fun to be there, and there is no joy in it. But it is absolutely necessary because without it, we cannot be trusted with what He has for us.

REBELLIOUS PEOPLE AND HURT PEOPLE BOTH LOOK THE SAME.

I can look back on times in my life, as far back as when I was seven years old, when God spoke to my heart about things in my life. Those decisions I made during my childhood and teenage years have brought me to where I am now. Decisions that I make now are going to affect me ten years from now.

Almost overnight Joseph had gone from being the son of the wealthiest man in the region to being a slave. How could this have happened to him? He was bought by Potiphar, and forced to serve in his household. Even though it wasn't right, or fair, he was diligent in his duties. He served faithfully. He wasn't guilty of any disloyalty or wrong, yet no one believed him.

Every time I appear on television, I get letters from prisoners who write asking for money to help them build their cases and get out of prison. Of course, they are not guilty; no one ever is.

The truth of the matter is that you can complain about the situation you are in. You can murmur about your husband, your job, your boss, your pastor and your church, or you can roll up your sleeves and rejoice. You can put your hand to the task with a good attitude, and you can get out of it. It's your choice. If you don't like where you are today, it's not God's fault.

Joseph had a right to fight and scream. He could have gotten angry and bitter, but even in his immaturity, God saw something in him that was very precious.

WOUNDS CAN LOOK LIKE REBELLION

I ministered to a young girl, and the things I had to share with her were tough. She was a guest in my home, so I used my advantage to speak into her life about her situation. As I spoke to her, she became very angry and got teary-eyed. I even thought she was going to take a poke at me. She cried after using the famous quote, "It's not fair."

"Maybe it wasn't fair," I explained, "but you have to extend to the other party the same grace that you expect to receive from God." I emphasized how others may not deserve grace, but neither did she. We talked further through her many tears.

Later I heard that when she told someone about our conversation, she said, "No one has ever gone that far. When other people see me getting upset and angry, they just walk away. My own mother shuts me down and walks away. Cathy was the first person who loved me while talking to me. That enabled me to receive it."

Rebellious people and hurt people both look the same. You'll never know the difference unless you spend time talking with them to find out what's inside of them. Wounded animals are going to protect the part of them that is hurt, and they will become vicious when the survival mechanism kicks in. A lot of people

73

in the body of Christ are very hurt and wounded. They appear to be rebels, sitting in the back of the church, chomping on gum, looking at their watches, daring you to bless them. They don't want to be there. But you never know what's really going on inside—not at first anyway. Time and again I have found that when

I THINK HE GOT A LITTLE TOO CLOSE TO THE FLAME, AND SHE WAS ABLE TO GET HOLD OF HIS COAT.

I'm finished speaking, those same hurt people break down and sob. In spite of what it looked like, they weren't rebellious; they were hurting. They just needed someone to love on them.

74

Joseph had been hurt by his brothers, thrown into an impossible situation, but he didn't strike out at others in his hurt. He did his job, and over and over again he proved himself faithful to Potiphar. As a result, he was rewarded by Potiphar, who promoted him, making him head of the whole household. The Word says that Potiphar didn't have to think about anything except to open his mouth and eat the food set before him. Talk about a faithful servant!

It didn't take long for Potiphar to see the loyalty in Joseph. If that quality is in you, others will see it very quickly. Employers tell us that one of the biggest problems with employees is their lack of loyalty. One day a McDonald's manager told me how he loves to hire senior citizens because they show up early, work their jobs diligently and demonstrate great work habits. Apparently seniors don't have chips on their shoulders. They've been though life, and they are not striving to own the place.

DON'T GET TOO CLOSE TO THE FIRE

Joseph was a young adult. He was promoted from within. But he also blew it in Potiphar's house. As we know, Potiphar's wife came to Joseph on a regular basis, trying to seduce him. She was beautiful, and Joseph was quite a stud. It would have been easy for him to give in to her advances. One day he ran from her, and she grabbed his jacket and cried, "Rape." Hell hath no fury like a woman scorned.

Joseph was faithful to Potiphar and couldn't be seduced. But I think we may have missed something. Why did he have to go to jail? Remember, she pulled his coat off of him. How did that happen? I think, and this is my opinion, that he got a little too close to the flame, and she was able to get hold of his coat.

I think pride had a little to do with it, too. Pride causes us to get a little too close to the line without actually crossing it and sinning. Joseph wasn't walking down the hall when his jacket fell off. I think he got a little too close and then put the brakes on almost too late. The fact that she was able to get hold of his jacket is proof. Maybe the other servants testified at Joseph's trial that Joseph and Potiphar's wife were alone together.

Now I know that you're thinking, *My Sunday school teacher didn't tell me that.*

75

Well, I know human nature. I'm trying to get you to overcome all your spiritual BS, which is your *spiritual belief system*. We believe a lot of things that someone else told us that aren't written in the Word. God knew Joseph wasn't ready for the position of leadership yet, and so Joseph wound up in prison.

THE PLACE OF PREPARATION

Could prison possibly be the place of preparation? Yikes!!

We know the end of Joseph's story. He could have shortened his prison sentence after a stellar ministry opportunity presented itself. Joseph gave accurate and critical counsel and used the opportunity to boost his gifted anointing for dream interpretation. "Tell it to me, and *I will give* the interpretation," he cried. "Only remember me when you get out of here and get me out, too. I don't deserve this." So he was stuck there two more years.

Two years later, a now humbled, tender, matured Joseph was asked to interpret a king's dream. He said, "Perhaps *God will be merciful and give* us the interpretation."

What happened in prison during those two critical years? The Word doesn't tell us, but Joseph probably came to terms with his life, accepted whatever fate God had for him and remained loyal. Then just that quickly, he was up and out of prison, and he had a new career—with benefits.

Trust me, precious, you will never be forgotten. You are much too valuable to your God. By faith, ask the Lord for grace to remain faithful.

CHAPTER 7

LOYALTY ISN'T JUST FOR BOY SCOUTS

y cheeks burned red. I told myself, *Do not cry, do not cry,* but I was helpless as tears filled my eyes and ran down my face. The accusations stung. The motives that were being attributed to Randi and me were outright lies. My accusers misinterpreted my emotional response as being a sign of the shame of being caught and the ugly truth of guilt.

Wrong! The response was simmering rage coupled with grave hurt as this man and his wife laid accusation upon accusation upon us. I looked at the office door. Only five steps and I could be gone, but I didn't dare move because it would just be another "sign" (as good godly Christians call it) of our rebellion.

We thought we were meeting them for coffee—at least that's what they had said. Instead, it was a tribunal that unfortunately ended a seven-year relationship and a gulf too wide to cross. I vaguely heard the words *unaccountable, church attendance* and *iniquitous.* Each word was a slap. We were not novices, having ministered full time for twenty-five years, eighteen of them as pastors. I knew all too well that their judgments of us on that day would be their failures of tomorrow.

Grieving and wounded, I determined to study God's holy, infallible Word on being a faithful and loyal servant. I want to leave a legacy that is rich and full with friends who could say that I was both faithful and loyal.

> Then David went to Mahanaim. And Absalom crossed over the Jordan, he and all the men of Israel with him. And Absalom made Amasa captain of the army instead of Joab. This Amasa was the son of a man whose name was Jithra, an Israelite, who had gone in to Abigail the daughter of Nahash, sister of Zeruiah, Joab's mother. So Israel

and Absalom encamped in the land of Gilead.

—2 SAMUEL 17:24–26

Who was Amasa? He was one of David's prized men. He was his head elder or deacon or associate pastor or minister of music. You get the picture? He was one of David's right-hand, most-loyal men. But when Absalom, David's own son, mounted his campaign against his father, Amasa defected from David to Absalom. *Amasa* literally means "burden." Further study finds that Amasa was David's nephew. Not only did David's son turn

REJECTION WILL KILL YOU IF YOU LET IT.

against him, but along with that, David's nephew was appointed over all of Absalom's troops against him.

Now this may not ring your bell and get your mind wondering, but this is a vitally important principle to understand in your walk with God. Absalom wanted to hurt his father, so in order to put the knife in David, he replaced Joab with David's own nephew.

Unfortunately, many people in this world can be bought. Sadly, there are even people in ministry who can be bought. You need to make the decision right now that you will never let this happen to you.

My daughter told me that a young man in a group called Plus One had been an original member of Backstreet Boys before they hit the big time. The Lord spoke to this young man and told him, "If you choose

81

this, you will lose out because I have other things for your life." He had to watch the Backstreet Boys rise to fame and become wealthy while he sat home. Now the new group, Plus One, a Christian group that he joined, has been featured on one of the soaps, singing the theme song.

I thought of the awesomeness of God. What must this young man have thought while he watched the original group go forward without him. All he had was a word from the Lord. Can you imagine what his friends thought?

Faithfulness and loyalty will cost you something. It may look as if those who don't deserve it are getting blessed. David had to watch his son and his nephew betray him.

REJECTION WON'T KILL YOU IF YOU DON'T LET IT

God can turn even the most heartbreaking experiences around. I saw this when I was engaged to a man whom I had met when he held a meeting in our church. We set the wedding date. But then suddenly, he disappeared. I didn't hear from him. I tried to call him, but I never got a reply. I thought I was going to have a nervous breakdown. I was all of nineteen years old and had a wedding dress, a veil and a missing fiancé.

The next thing I heard was that he had met someone else and was going to be married. I went into such a depression, and the shock of it made me ill. Rejection will kill you if you let it. I never heard of him again, or the family singing group.

Three years later God sent me the most amazing man of God in the world. As I look back, if I had married that first man, I would have missed what God had for my life. I am saying this for someone who needs it. It's never too late. My experience hurt me so badly, but only for a while. Don't let anyone tell you that following Jesus does not have a price associated with it. Yes, there are hard places, and you will go through rejection, but it will only be for a season. It's

AS LONG AS YOU WON'T QUIT, THERE IS STILL HOPE FOR YOU—EVEN THOUGH IT HURTS.

like cauterizing something. It's painful, but unless you allow God to do it, you will die spiritually.

If I had not met Randi Lechner, I would not be in the ministry I am in today. I know beyond a shadow of a doubt that he opened up doors for things I knew nothing about. I followed behind him, because at that time I knew nothing of the prophetic.

What if I had married the other man? Would there have been hope for me? Absolutely. You may say, "What about me? I did just that." I will tell you this, God is a God of new beginnings. I don't mean you are to leave your husband, no, no, no. I don't care what has happened. The pastor's wife in Sydney, whose husband left her with three-week-old twins, thought her life was over. Yet God sent an awesome man of God to her, and now they are married, have a child together

83

and are serving as pastors of a large church.

The devil will try to tell you that it's too late, you're too old, you're too young or you've missed it. He's a liar. He is just trying to get you to stop. He wants you to quit. As long as you won't quit, there is still hope for you—even though it hurts.

Loyalty Goes Deeper Than Faithfulness

It says in 2 Samuel 19:8–13:

> Then the king arose and sat in the gate. And they told all the people, saying, "There is the king, sitting in the gate." So all the people came before the king. For everyone of Israel had fled to his tent.
>
> Now all the people were in a dispute throughout all the tribes of Israel, saying, "The king saved us from the hand of our enemies, he delivered us from the hand of the Philistines, and now he has fled from the land because of Absalom. But Absalom, whom we anointed over us, has died in battle. Now therefore, why do you say nothing about bringing back the king?"
>
> So King David sent to Zadok and Abiathar the priests, saying, "Speak to the elders of Judah, saying, 'Why are you the last to bring the king back to his house, since the words of all Israel have come to the king, to his very house? You are my brethren, you are my bone and my flesh. Why then are you the last to bring back the king?' And say to Amasa, 'Are you not my bone and my flesh? God do so to me, and more also, if you are not commander of the army before me continually in place of Joab.'"

Can you imagine David saying this? David told his nephew, "I know what you did. I know you went and served my son. I know you sold out, but I am going to pardon you and raise you up to be my commander-in-chief." That's real forgiveness. Can you do that to people who have wounded you? There is a big difference between loyalty and faithfulness—but David had both. It is possible to have one and not the other. For example, a wife can be faithful to her husband by not committing

WHEN YOU ARE A RECIPIENT OF MERCY, IT'S EASIER TO GIVE MERCY.

adultery, but then she can still be disloyal to him when she tells everyone who will listen, "I live with such a jerk. He won't go to church. He's mean and hateful." That is being faithful, but not loyal.

85

I know people who are faithful to their churches every week, but they are not loyal to them. They show up every Sunday and Wednesday, but they are not loyal. Loyalty has to do with the heart. Faithfulness is showing up bodily, but loyalty goes deeper. Loyalty requires that you make a decision to go deeper or not.

When Absalom died, David was stricken with grief, even though his son had betrayed him. Why was David able to give mercy to Amasa? Because David remembered when he had slept with Bathsheba. When you are the recipient of much mercy, you give mercy. He had stolen Uriah's wife and gotten her pregnant. When she became pregnant, he tried to get rid of her, dump her and reject her. He was also a murderer because he had her husband killed. Then he married her. He got himself in a real mess.

When you are a recipient of mercy, it's easier to give mercy. People who don't give mercy become judgmental. Then in their time of need, they find it very difficult to receive mercy. When you are always the one to say you're sorry, even if you think you are right, the blessing and the favor of God will be on your life. God will raise you up higher. Don't use religious, false humility.

TESTS WILL ALWAYS COME KNOCKING ON YOUR DOOR

If you think you are not going to have trials and tests in this life, you are in for a surprise. All the well-known television preachers you admire so much, as wonderful as they are, have their share of problems. Not everyone likes them or agrees with their ministries. Some of them must even have bodyguards to protect them from people who are angry with them and would do them harm.

There will always be someone who doesn't like you and doesn't believe in what you are doing. Don't use the time or effort to fight them. I always say that you don't need to make excuses and defend yourself—your friends don't need it, and your enemies won't believe it.

The people of Israel were disloyal to David—they deserted him.

> And there happened to be there a rebel, whose name was Sheba the son of Bichri, a Benjamite. And he blew a trumpet, and said: "We have no share in David, nor do we have inheritance in the

son of Jesse; every man to his tent, O Israel!" So every man deserted David, and followed Sheba the son of Bichri.

—2 SAMUEL 20:1–2

YOU DON'T NEED TO MAKE EXCUSES AND DEFEND YOUR-SELF—YOUR FRIENDS DON'T NEED IT, AND YOUR ENEMIES WON'T BELIEVE IT.

The people all deserted David and followed Sheba. After all, Sheba had a trumpet. People will follow whoever will stand up and make a loud noise. After all, people are followers. Be careful whom you follow. Being wealthy is no substitute for God's favor.

"But the men of Judah, from the Jordan as far as Jerusalem, remained loyal to their king" (v. 2). They did what? Yes, they remained loyal. Scripture doesn't say they remained *faithful*; it says they remained *loyal*.

After the death of his son Absalom, David returned home to Jerusalem:

> Now David came to his house at Jerusalem. And the king took the ten women, his concubines whom he had left to keep the house, and put them in seclusion and supported them, but did

87

not go in to them. So they were shut up to the day of their death, living in widowhood.

—2 SAMUEL 20:3

Isn't that a shame? Do you know why that happened to them? Because David's son had slept with them, and David was an honorable man.

DOING IT YOUR OWN WAY IS DANGEROUS

And the king said to Amasa, "Assemble the men of Judah for me within three days, and be present here yourself." So Amasa went to assemble the men of Judah. But he delayed longer than the set time which David had appointed him.

—2 SAMUEL 20:4

This is important: David knew that time was of the essence, so he commanded Amasa to gather the troops from Judah within three days. Because of the threat of Sheba, David needed to get the army together as quickly as possible. Amasa may have thought he was being loyal by taking the extra time to gather more troops, but he didn't obey David's instruction.

You may say, "So what?" But just hang on. The Word tells us that David said that Sheba would do more harm than Absalom. God told David to take his men and pursue Sheba lest he find fortified cities and escape from David's army. So they went out to do the pursuing. When they found Sheba, Amasa came before them. Joab was dressed in battle armor with a nice big sword fastened to him. As he was going forward, it fell out of the sheath. Joab asked Amasa if he was in good health. I guess that's the same as our "How are you?" When Joab took Amasa by the beard to kiss him, Amasa didn't notice the sword in Joab's hand. The sword struck Amasa in his stomach, and he died on the spot.

ONCE YOU GET A REPUTATION THAT YOU CAN'T BE TRUSTED, IT TAKES YEARS TO REBUILD YOUR REPUTATION.

Then Joab and his brother Abishai chased after Sheba. One of Joab's men stood near Amasa and asked that all those who favored Joab and were for David to follow Joab. They had to move Amasa out of the way and cover him up because all David's men had gathered around him. When they moved Amasa to the side of the road, the men moved on and followed Joab in his pursuit of Sheba.

Amasa's body was like a distraction on the highway. You've seen cars go by an accident and do what we call rubber-necking. That's what these soldiers were doing. You may say it doesn't seem fair that Amasa died. But remember, he had sown seeds of disloyalty. David said to take three days, but he decided he had a better way of doing things.

It drives me crazy in my office when I ask people to do something, and I have a reason for wanting it a certain way, but they think they have a better way

89

because I haven't told them the whole plan. Then they get angry with me when I ask them why they didn't do it the way I had asked them to. They often say, "I didn't think it made that much difference." It's important to remember that the way we serve those whom God has given to us is the way that we will serve God.

As I was gathering my thoughts for this book, my mind went to the time when they were carrying the ark of the covenant. They were instructed not to touch it. As it began to shift, one of the men reached out to steady it, and he dropped dead. I always thought, *That stinks. He was doing God a favor. He didn't want the ark to fall.* But then the Lord said to me, "That wasn't the point. I had a way of doing it, and I said, 'Don't touch it.'"

Not following orders is what cost Amasa his life. David had to launch an attack against Sheba because he felt he was going to do more damage to his kingdom than his son Absalom had done to it. Sheba, to whom someone had given a trumpet, got a lot of people to follow him. David was waiting for Amasa to gather the troops. David told him to do it within three days. He was in a desperate situation. He had no troops except the household troops. He wanted his field troops, but now instead he had to send the troops that were in the palace.

In this desperate situation, he had to take the men who guarded his family. He wanted to use Amasa, but found he couldn't trust him. Once you get a reputation that you can't be trusted, it takes years to rebuild your reputation. You probably still remember the girl who got pregnant in high school. Jimmy Swaggart and Jim Bakker will be tag lines for the late night talk shows until Jesus comes. It's a shame and a tragedy, but that's what happens. People do not forget for a long time.

Amasa had a bad reputation, and David couldn't

trust him. Now he gave him a job to do, and he didn't know where he was. (Maybe he joined Sheba because he liked his trumpet.)

VESSELS OF HONOR ARE TRUSTWORTHY

So David gathered his household troops and sent them. If someone asks you to do something, can that

LOYALTY IS MORE IMPORTANT THAN YOUR OPINION.

person relax, knowing you will follow his request? Can you be trusted to follow through as instructed and do the whole task to the end no matter what it takes?

I am absolutely amazed by some of the things that happen at places where I minister. At some churches they won't let me carry my purse, my briefcase (not that I'm above all that) or my suitcase. On the other hand, I have also been to places where the pastor drives off and leaves me at the church by myself. I was at a conference not long ago where I was to leave that church when the confusion was over and go to another conference. The pastor that was to pick me up wasn't there on time, and the pastor of the church sponsoring the first conference just left me standing in the lobby by myself. He and the others with him were about to drive off and leave me alone, when suddenly they realized I was alone with nowhere to go. Actually, I was about to call the airlines and go back home.

91

Sadly, we don't teach ethics anymore. Many people are not trained properly in our society. Ethics are supposed to be taught at home. Parents should be teaching their children about faithfulness and loyalty. Instead, people are told, "If you don't like that marriage, get out of it." The same is said about jobs and churches.

Amasa never learned; he continued to do it his own way. I've heard people say, "You just ought to be glad that I showed up." We should not have a *volunteer* attitude. We are not *volunteers*; we are *servants*.

When I hire people to work in my house to help with the children, I tell them right off the bat, "This is not Dillards. This is not a job. This is a ministry. You don't punch in or out, and you may be called on to work on weekends. This house is a house of ministry. The minute you lose that focus, you are not any good to anyone. You will be discontented, mad and frustrated. This is a high-stress job. But on the other hand, I pay very well. I am very generous with you. When I go somewhere and receive a little extra, I will pass on the money to you. I will remember your birthday and be a good employer to you. I will treat you the way God blesses me. I do not expect just faithfulness—I want loyalty. We

92

LOYALTY MEANS YOU WANT THE ONE YOU SERVE TO BE BLESSED.

are going to yell at each other and be like any other family. But I don't want you to go out of here and discuss me and my husband and our ministry."

I asked my husband if we could get our employees to sign a confidentiality agreement as they do in Hollywood. He asked what purpose would it serve. Well, I thought we could go to court if someone broke our agreement. But he let me know that the Word says we can't sue Christians. I said, "Well, we could scare them."

He casually answered me with this astounding statement, "If we hire someone who has the disposition to talk about us, it doesn't matter what they sign; they will talk about us anyway." Now that's comforting, isn't it? Oh well, we do a lot of praying before we hire anyone, and we trust God.

Loyalty was more important than Amasa's opinion. Loyalty is more important than your opinion. You may be asked to do something that you think is absolutely stupid. You could probably think of a hundred different better ways to do the same thing. People who think like that will always be a big duck in a little pond. There are so many Christians with tremendous gifts and talents and anointing, but God will never be able to use them. The reason is that they know how to be faithful, but they have never learned the lesson of loyalty.

What does loyalty look like? We know what it doesn't look like, but what does it look like? *Loyalty* means you want the one you serve to be blessed. I'm not only talking about people; I'm talking about God. Some Christians are faithful to God, but they are not loyal to Him.

NOW ABOUT YOUR SPOUSE...

The greatest place to test loyalty is in your own marriage. You may think that your mate doesn't deserve your loyalty. Maybe he or she was unfaithful to you, or

93

maybe he or she is a jerk. All of us have people in our lives who are the sandpaper of the Holy Spirit.

Let's look at Genesis 24:1–4:

> Now Abraham was old, well advanced in age; and the LORD had blessed Abraham in all things. So Abraham said to the oldest servant of his house, who ruled over all that he had, "Please, put your hand under my thigh, and I will make you swear by the LORD, the God of heaven and the God of earth, that you will not take a wife for my son from the daughters of the Canaanites, among whom I dwell; but you shall go to my country and to my family, and take a wife for my son Isaac."

Abraham had another son, Ishmael, but he was concerned about his son of promise. The selection of a wife for Isaac, who would provide an heir, was vital, but Abraham was old and could not do this himself. He had to trust that his servant would think as he thought and do as he would do. This is the whole purpose of mentoring. Mentoring encourages you to depart from thinking the way you would think and instead to think the way God thinks. Your mentor should not be someone that you like a lot. It should be someone who has an understanding of the way God thinks and enables you to change your stinkin' thinkin' to God's thinking.

We get in trouble when we don't think as God thinks. That's why people get mad at God and get depressed, discouraged, despondent, despaired and lose their joy. They don't have anyone speaking into their lives and helping them to see how God thinks about the situation. If you will only change the way you think, you will not be miserable anymore.

94

In Genesis 24:5–9, we read that the worried servant told Abraham:

WE GET IN TROUBLE WHEN WE DON'T THINK AS GOD THINKS.

"Perhaps the woman will not be willing to follow me to this land. Must I take your son back to the land from which you came?" But Abraham said to him, "Beware that you do not take my son back there. The LORD God of heaven, who took me from my father's house and from the land of my family, and who spoke to me and swore me, saying, 'To your descendants I give this land,' He will send His angel before you, and you shall take a wife for my son from there. And if the woman is not willing to follow you, then you will be released from this oath; only do not take my son back there." So the servant put his hand under the thigh of Abraham his master, and swore to him concerning this matter.

95

What was the servant doing? He was evidently in fear. I think he would have liked to have a backup plan. And the Word says:

Then the servant took ten of his master's camels and departed, for all his master's goods were in his hand. And he arose and went to Mesopotamia, to the city of Nahor. And he made his camels kneel down outside the city by a well of water at evening time, the time when women go to draw water. Then he said, "O LORD God of my master Abraham, please give me success this day, and show kindness to my master Abraham."

—GENESIS 24:10–12

SOMETIMES WE HAVE TO WATER CAMELS—THEY ARE NOT KIND, AND THEY DO NOT SAY THANK YOU.

He was loyal because he wanted to bless the one he served. In this, he blessed the man that he served, but he also blessed the God that he served. Loyalty is driven by love to bless others.

In verses 13–15 we read:

> "Behold, here I stand by the well of water, and the daughters of the men of the city are coming out to draw water. Now let it be that the young woman to whom I say, 'Please let down your pitcher that I may drink,' and she says, 'Drink, and I will also give your camels a drink'—let her be the one You have appointed for Your servant Isaac. And by this I will know that You have shown kindness to my master." And it happened, before he had finished speaking.

96

Isn't that awesome? When you are loyal, God will answer you before the words are out of your mouth. You see, we say we don't serve God for the blessing, but I want you to know that He blesses you. When you are loyal to Him, He blesses you before the words are out of your mouth. He will do so much for you that you won't have room enough to contain it.

Just at that moment, right at the exact time, you will intersect with the will of God. That is what happened to Rebekah.

> And it happened, before he had finished speaking, that behold, Rebekah, who was born to Bethuel, son of Milcah, the wife of Nahor, Abraham's brother, came out with her pitcher on her shoulder. Now the young woman was very beautiful to behold, a virgin; no man had known her. And she went down to the well, filled her pitcher, and came up.
>
> And the servant ran to meet her and said, "Please let me drink a little water from your pitcher." So she said, "Drink, my lord." Then she quickly let her pitcher down to her hand, and gave him a drink.
>
> —GENESIS 24:15–18

97

But Rebekah didn't leave after she gave Abraham's servant a drink. In verses 19 and 20 we read that she quickly offered to draw water for his camels. This got the attention of that old servant:

> And the man, wondering at her, remained silent as to know whether the LORD had made his journey prosperous or not.
>
> —GENESIS 24:21

I am convinced that if that servant had been a mortal Holy Spirit he would have said, "OK, you've passed the test. You were willing to do it." But instead, he sat there until she had finished watering all of the camels. A mortal Holy Spirit might have said, "I don't want to put anybody out. I just wanted to see if you were willing." Sometimes we have to go ahead and water camels. Camels that are coming out of the desert are really thirsty. They are not kind, and they do not say thank you. Camels are mean, stinky and dirty, and they fight their masters. They are not nice.

Your destiny might be wrapped up in a bunch of stinky, dirty, nasty camels. The servant asked Rebekah who her father was. She invited him home with her. And we know the rest of that wonderful story.

The focal point was for Abraham's faithful, loyal servant to please his master—not just get the job done. He had nothing to gain personally.

So What Does Loyalty Look Like?

98

Let me tell you what loyalty looks like. Loyalty means that the one you serve can trust you. I think that someone telling me they trust me is the greatest compliment anyone could ever pay me. Trust means that you will not only to do the task, but that you are supportive, you are looking out for the other person's interest, and you are thinking like them.

Loyalty means you serve the way you have been asked to. If someone asks you to put out the blue plates, you don't put out the red ones instead because you think they look better. If we could ask Amasa, I think he would say, "But I thought it would have been better to bring more troops. I just thought…"

Everyone shows up at a new ministry with a new building. Everyone likes to come in when everything is established and there is a good youth and music program. But who wants to hang in there when the going gets rough?

LOYALTY MEANS YOU SERVE THE WAY YOU HAVE BEEN ASKED TO.

According to John 13:1, loyalty means exactly that. A leader hangs in there even when the going gets rough.

> Now before the Feast of the Passover, when Jesus knew that His hour had come that He should depart from this world to the Father, having loved His own who were in the world, *He loved them to the end.*
>
> **—JOHN 13:1, EMPHASIS ADDED**

Jesus loved His disciples and all people still when He was on the cross. Even while He was in horrible pain, He was concerned about those who loved Him and followed Him. He knew they didn't understand. He knew they thought He was going to set up an earthly kingdom. Rather than hollering for morphine or yelling at the people for what they were doing to Him, He was thinking about serving. When He was wounded, in pain and being betrayed, He was thinking about others. He was concerned for His mother. He asked John to take care of her.

Loyalty means the leader hangs in there when the going gets rough. Your loyalty must lie between you, the Lord and your people. Your loyalty must not be to yourself. It can't be a time for asking, "What's in this for me?" God will reward you. He will bless you.

LOYALTY DESCRIBES A HEART-SET THAT IS POSITIVE, HONORING THE ONE SERVED AND GIVING WITHOUT SELF-SERVING MOTIVES.

I can't number the people who have come to me and said that the Lord told them they were to be a part of my ministry. When I hear that, I take about three steps backward, because I know their statement must be tried and tested to see how long they will hang in there.

Loyalty and faithfulness are interchangeable, but there is an important difference. *Faithfulness* refers to action. If you give a person a task and he performs it properly, then he is faithful. But that does not say anything about his heart or motive.

Loyalty describes a heart-set that is positive, honoring the one served and giving without self-serving motives. Loyalty does not say, "I'm doing this for what I can get out of it. Maybe I'll get to sit on the platform." I'm sure you've heard this saying, "You scratch my back, and I'll scratch yours."

I may be stepping on some toes, but I often hear associate pastors say that they have served in one place long enough and now they deserve more. Even though God has called them to that position, they get big in their own eyes because people are telling them how wonderful they are. They get ahead of God, thinking it's time to have their own following, only to have it all fall flat. Why? Because the anointing they had came from being under that senior pastor. But they misread it and thought the anointing was their own.

First Corinthians 13:5–6 says that love "does not behave rudely, does not seek its own, is not provoked, thinks no evil; does not rejoice in iniquity, but rejoices in the truth." This is especially applicable to relationships. A wife can be faithful to her husband, but despise him and talk negatively about him to other people. Then she wonders why he doesn't want to come to church or get saved. She has uncovered him before the whole church. Why would he want to go to her church with her?

We all have friends that we go to with personal problems. Everyone needs someone they can talk to, confide in and pray with. However, don't make the mistake of running down your family before others.

We are faithful to Jesus because He is our Master and our Lord. We are loyal to Him because He is our Brother and our Friend. There is much joy in being loyal. You get a crown.

This will tie everything I've said together. John 3:27 says that a man cannot receive anything unless it is given to him from heaven. John 3:28–29 continues:

> You yourselves bear me witness, that I said, "I am

not the Christ" but, "I have been sent before Him." He who has the bride is the bridegroom; but the friend of the bridegroom, who stands and hears him, rejoices greatly because of the bridegroom's voice. Therefore this joy of mine is fulfilled. He must increase, but I must decrease.

THAT'S HOW YOU GET THE GLORY. YOU HAVE TO DIE. HE NEVER MADE YOU TO OCCUPY THE SAME SPACE THAT HE OCCUPIES.

DEATH TO THE FLESH FIRST, THEN HIS GLORY

102

I have shared with you how God is setting before us an open heaven. We are living in an exciting hour—God is doing so much for us. John the Revelator talks about heaven. He is excited when he describes all the jewels. That heavenly stuff is "the things" that are worth putting all of your hopes in. Our whole society today is based on gold, but gold is actually worthless when compared to what is really important. God is paving streets from gold. We are going to walk on gold. John tried to describe it.

We talk about fire and glory meetings. But compared to the glory of God, those meetings are just good "tingly" meetings. When confronted with God's glory, John exclaimed that his body was not wired to contain it. He physically felt that he was going to die if God revealed any more glory.

That's how you get the glory. You have to die. He never made you to occupy the same space that He occupies. Your flesh and His glory cannot exist together. The more loyal you are to God, and the closer you get to Him, the more He will pour out His glory and the more your flesh will die.

So if your flesh is dying, rejoice. You're getting more glory. He says you are going from glory to glory and faith to faith. This means that your faith is increasing because the glory is coming. However, there is no room for His glory until your flesh dies.

God once told me, "Cathy, the whole idea was that I wanted your flesh to die. That was My whole purpose. If your flesh goes, then I can occupy the space. That's why there are some people who will never get it." Let's face it, sin is fun for a season. Some will hold on to fear because they believe they must be in control. God tells us to let go so that He can fill us with His glory.

Wherever His glory is, He will increase. Be faithful, but add loyalty to your faithfulness. I pray for you today that God will seal this word in your heart and you will possess something so much greater than you have ever had.

103

CHAPTER 8

"JUST CLAIM IT" AND OTHER STUPID SAYINGS

I do not recall ever seeing such pure childlike excitement. The words tumbled out of his mouth as he showed me the treasure in his hand. No, it was not one of my sons with a pet frog or a new matchbox car. It was my dad, and the incident happened only two and a half years ago.

Cut carefully from the newspaper was the drawing of a house. It was the kind that the Sunday *Tribune* runs with three different floor plans and names like "The Aspen" or "The Ryecatcher" or the "Four Closets the Size of a Bedroom." The one my father had cut out was a three-bedroom, two-bath house. It was brand-new and ready to be constructed.

He said to me, "Cathy, this house is what I want. The Lord asked me if I could believe Him for this house. I asked your mother if she could believe with me, and she said that she definitely could. In addition, He told me to print a sign that reads *Jehovah Jireh* and place it over the door of the sketch."

Like a little boy full of excitement, he opened his hand to reveal the prize. The newspaper clipping had *Jehovah Jireh* printed over the door of "The Aspen," just as the Lord told him to do.

The newspaper clipping with the floor plans of this moderately priced house found a prominent place on my dad's refrigerator door. It was fastened there with an ugly magnet, which I am sure was made by the Women's Ministry gals as a fundraiser. The magnet was a little blue man constructed from paper towels. One eye was missing, and his waist was tied with a piece of brown yarn.

How appropriate! A fantasy house held in place by a one-eyed fantasy man. I nodded my head and uttered the prerequisite, religious intonation, "Amen, Daddy; I'm standing with you."

Secretly, my heart was breaking. Mom and Dad were living in a nice three-bedroom apartment. The arrangement was partly to be near us and partly so Dad could receive his chemotherapy treatments from the nearby Mayo Clinic. He was battling esophageal and liver cancer, and the prognosis was not good.

Now he wanted a house, his *Jehovah Jireh* home, which he felt in his heart that God had prepared to bless him with. His present situation was tenuous, yet my precious daddy, at sixty-seven years of age, wanted to build a future.

That day I sat in the car outside his apartment and wept. My father had said yes to the call of God upon his life as a teenager. He and Mom had worked and ministered throughout all of their married lives. Now they lived in a borrowed house, made car payments to the bank and brought in a little over $900 a month in social security.

The day Daddy died, I was sitting in his Lazy Boy chair in his apartment. Everyone was talking, crying and making the appropriate arrangements. Although I was listening, I did not really hear what was going on. My eyes wandered to the piece of newspaper, which was still attached to the refrigerator door. The faded edges had begun to curl.

107

Everything inside of me wanted to scream, "All he wanted was a house! The 1,562-square-foot Aspen. Now he is gone, and the promise died with him." Somehow, none of it seemed fair to me.

Just that very day I had read that Clint Eastwood, the exact same age as my dad, had a baby girl with his new wife. I thought the paper said they had a house *in Aspen*. For all I knew, he probably *owned* Aspen.

In addition, Sean Connery came out with a new

movie that week. He was going to be knighted by Queen Elizabeth. He was also the same age as my dad. Sean Connery had homes in the Bahamas, Spain, Scotland and probably had the Aspen II floor plan.

HIS PRESENT WAS TENUOUS, YET MY PRECIOUS DADDY, AT 67 YEARS OF AGE, WANTED TO BUILD A FUTURE.

You might wonder, dear reader, how I know all of these things. Well, I file them in a special place in my brain called "useless information and nonessential *National Enquirer*-type stuff," which religious people say they do not care about but anyone with children needs to know. Moreover, teens are extremely impressed with any Christian who has seen any movie besides *A Thief in the Night*.

A Date With Destiny

In one of our conversations about nothing, which last about an hour twice a day, my mom mentioned to me that she had run into a friend of hers who had been a member of my parents' church in 1972 in another part of the state.

They had lost contact with each other through the years and could not believe they were now living in the same city. Much had changed during those years. Mom had been a widow now for one and a half years, and her friend had remarried. "Carol is in real estate now," my mom told me.

"That's nice," I answered with the sort of interest one has in dust mites. How very selfish of me. If it does not affect my world, then why bother talking about it?

Several lunches and heart-to-heart talks later, Mom told me that she was going to look at a house. Now I really wanted to have faith, but the fact remained that Mom had no money, I had no money and my brothers had no money—at least not the kind to buy your mother a house. Clint Eastwood has money. Sean Connery has money. Excuse me, I mean SIR Sean Connery. Usually I am the one with the great faith— the leap-over-the-mountain, step-across-the-line and put-the-devil-under-my-feet kind of faith.

"Mom, does Carol know we don't have any money?" I inquired of her.

"Oh, yes. She says that they can work out a deal where I can get the house without money. In fact, I wouldn't be surprised if the bank paid me to buy the house!" And she laughed about it! Can you imagine? I chalked it up to progressive real-estate talk.

Two weeks later, Mom excitedly called me from her cell phone. Of course, she has to talk fast because her cell phone only gives her $8.00 worth of free words a month, or so it seems. "Are you sitting down, Honey?"

"Yes," I lied.

"I just looked at some land and a house plan. I have to go now, because I'm out of cell phone words."

"OK, bye, Mom," I responded, as I stood there thinking about this strange conversation and wondering what just took place.

109

AMAZING, BUT TRUE

What happened is so wonderful, so powerful and so encouraging that my publishing house and I accept no responsibility for any physical harm—self-inflicted or otherwise—for your "glory fit" after reading the incredible following account.

THE WORD OF GOD IS SO POWERFUL THAT EVEN AFTER A MAN DIES, GOD MUST FULFILL HIS PROMISE TO HIS SERVANT.

One Saturday afternoon, Mom took my brother and sister-in-law to see her little plot of land where she hoped that one day before Y3K takes place she would build a home.

They walked around the "land," which took approximately six seconds, three seconds each way. She then took them to the office so they could see a picture of what the "finished project" would look like.

The wonderful Christian couple in the office casually asked her if she would like to see the brand-new house across the street that was finished and ready to be occupied. It was bigger than the one she was going to have built. Evidently, the couple who built the house lost their financing, so it would be available if she was interested.

With the help of her precious realtor friend, Carol,

and faster than you can say, "Mama's got a brand-new house," my semi-mature mother bought, closed on and moved into her brand-new house—in three weeks time!

A week before the closing, Mom took me by the house on the way home from the airport. I had just arrived in Jacksonville after a brutal three-day conference. I was weary, a little discouraged and a lot disappointed, which was pretty much normal for me.

Mom slowly drove into the development with brand-new homes lining the streets. Landscaping, still in infancy, was the common bond between these new land barons. With all the suspense and pride of a new mother showing off her long-awaited firstborn, she carefully drove into the driveway and looked at my face for any reaction to her new addition. Sitting in front of the lovely home with its beautiful pale yellow vinyl lap siding and trimmed in fresh white paint with a pristine door just installed and waiting to greet its new family, I fell silent.

Mother was already out of the car and looking for the errant workman who had left the garage door open. I did not move. I could not move, for facing me was "The Aspen." The tears welled up, filled my eyes and spilled down my cheeks. "Oh, Daddy," I cried softly as I buried my face in my hands.

Realizing that I was not behind her, Mom came back to the car to find me. Misinterpreting my tears, she tapped on the window and asked, "What's wrong, Honey? Do you think I made a mistake and this is not God's will?"

She searched my face for approval, just as I had done all of my life with every decision and at every crossroad. When I needed a tender heart or an encouraging word, the elusive parental blessing was what I sought after.

"No, Mommy. It's just that this is the house, Dad's house, the newspaper house, the *Jehovah Jireh* house. Do you realize that when Daddy cut that house out of the paper, named it and started believing for it, it was not even built? The land wasn't even developed yet."

HOW MARVELOUS! HOW WONDERFUL! AND MY SONG SHALL EVER BE...

He asked, prayed and then obeyed. I do not remember hearing him shout, yell or scream, "I CLAIM IT! I CLAIM IT!" He just cut it out of paper, named it and stuck it on the refrigerator. And yet the Word of God is so powerful that even after a man dies, God *must* fulfill His promise to His servant.

I thought of my dad's favorite song.

112

> I stand amazed in the presence
> Of Jesus the Nazarene,
> And wonder how He could love me,
> A sinner, condemned, unclean.
>
> How marvelous! How wonderful!
> And my song shall ever be:
> How marvelous! How wonderful
> Is my Savior's love for me!*

He would make this song a part of the worship service as often as possible. I can still see him waving his arms back and forth as though he were leading ten thousand people in the congregation instead of fifty. His voice was the loudest as he exuberantly sang this as his testimony.

When I graduated from high school, my father was asked to speak for baccalaureate and was given the privilege of choosing the hymn for the graduating class of 1972. He submitted that song, "My Savior's Love," which was his favorite.

There were protests from the music department heads and school board members because this was a predominately Lutheran and Brethren community. No one had ever heard of "My Savior's Love." Dad stuck to his guns. It was his only daughter's graduation, and we *would* have an upbeat, encouraging, albeit unknown-to-them, song. I winced when I overheard conversation among my fellow students about how Cathy Rothert's dad would be messing up our baccalaureate.

When my father finished preaching that night, the auditorium, which was packed to capacity, was silent. Most of them had never witnessed the power of God's anointing on a preacher who was not just a minister.

The organ began to play the introduction to Dad's hymn. I felt as though I alone was helping my dad as we raised our voices, singing of our Savior's love. By the time we sang the last verse, the whole congregation was on its feet. Everyone was singing with a loud voice:

How marvelous! How wonderful! And my song shall ever be...

It was a personal triumph for me. After all, I was only seventeen years old!

At graduation the next day, students and teachers alike were humming and whistling the melody that, without realizing it, had imbedded itself into their hearts. It had become an anthem to a bunch of high

113

school kids that God's marvelous love was even more wonderful than "Nearer, My God, to Thee."

Dad never said another word about it because that was his way. It never found its way into his newsletter, tape-of-the-month or to a television program (oh, well, if he had one)!

Now, looking at this house it seemed as if the windows and doors became a face smiling at me. The house was his final crown here on earth, not a mansion over the hilltop, but the Aspen in Jacksonville for his sweetheart, his wife, his widow. A Jehovah Jireh house for his family and for all who would enter to hear this story of God's faithfulness and be healed. Eat your hearts out, Clint and Sean, for *this* is joy, faith, hope and love at its best. Thank You, Jesus, and thank you, Carol!

114

---

*"My Savior's Love" by Charles H. Gabriel. Public domain.

CHAPTER 9

PLEASE TELL ME THAT'S NOT PERMANENT MARKER

(AN EXPOSÉ ON WHAT WE ONLY THINK IS PERMANENT)

e have a darling two-year-old daughter, Hadassah Rose, whom I love to dress up in Battenburg lace dresses, hair sleekly pulled up into a bushy little puff ball. We tie it all up with a matching lace bow and pull little tendrils of hair loose to frame her face and dangle down her short little neck.

Her face is soft, and she is still a pudgy baby. Strangers stop us in church, at the store or McDonald's and "ooh" and "aah," telling her how adorable she is.

This is precisely the moment when our glorious, exquisite two-year-old goes totally silent. Her eyes roll upward and into a fixed position and rapidly dilate. It may be my overactive imagination, but she begins to groan like Bill Bixby when he morphs into the Incredible Hulk.

No one sees what happens next except the eagle-eye trained mother of this exquisite china doll. Slowly, a string of saliva drools out of the corner of her mouth. The end result is a ball of spit on the floor of Wal-Mart, McDonald's, the church nursery or my family room. She can, after all, spit at equal opportunity.

No, Hadassah is not having a seizure, at least the medical kind, and she does not need deliverance ala Linda Blair. She is just registering her displeasure in whatever her little two-and-a-half-year-old brain deems displeasing to her. Hadassah spits when too many people pay attention to her.

She also spits when overlooked (ignored) or told to eat broccoli. If she does not care for your choice of shoes for her feet for the day, my ever style-conscious daughter spits on or near them. She will then retrieve the purple and yellow flowered sandals that you had packed away in a box marked "stuff three sizes too small" or "hideous and intended for Botswana."

Because you are just too tired to argue, you cram her little chubby feet into the shoes, knowing very well that Dr. James Dobson would not approve.

It is the exact same reason that you allowed her to wear her Barney bathing suit with her 101 Dalmatians socks and big sister's gold Mary Jane Christmas shoes to the grocery store. I know that I need counseling, but in Botswana they might think that was rather attractive.

I cannot believe that I have morphed into this! My children used to adhere to the "Jacqueline Kennedy School of Fashionable Dress." The highest priority was making sure that dresses were starched and shirts tucked into cream slacks with matched socks and deck shoes. Noses were wiped and diaper bags fully stocked with only appropriate brands. Now my slogan is, "Does anyone have a wet wipe?"

A stranger replies, "Yes, but it's been used, only once."

"Great, I'll take it," I say while wondering which end of her leaking child it was used on.

I idolized my mother's generation of women. You remember the petite, blonde, Doris Day types, dressed in pink, crisp, shirtwaist dresses with white aprons. The dress even had a Betty Crocker ruffle in the back. Now I, for one, refuse to put a big bow on my backside.

Do you remember Aunt Bea? Well, she is what kindly grandmothers are supposed to look like. You know, the gray hair, gray dress and gray shoes. Did it just seem that way because we had a black-and-white television?

Who can forget the day that Jacqueline Kennedy stood in Arlington Cemetery with Caroline and John-John? Please forgive my shallowness here, but even as an eight-and-a-half-year-old little girl, I could not take my eyes off those matching blue coats. Caroline's was princess cut, and John wore a Chesterfield. Both of them had white socks with matching brown shoes. For two years I tried to dress my little brother, Harold Randall, like John-John. My cost-efficient and fashion-free father kept buzzing his hair with clippers from Sears. Mom bought him Wrangler jeans, and the child insisted on wearing a Deputy Dawg sweatshirt that had been donated to the missionary barrel. Come on, people; work with me here!

Image is a very powerful weapon. We choose hairstyles, cars, clothing, schools (the uniforms) and even churches to identify who we are or who we want people to *think* we are.

Have you not ever once looked at a young woman who walked into a restaurant with long, thick hair, perfect makeup, skin-tight leather, knee-high boots, and as you looked her over thought to yourself, *But is she really happy?* My opinion is, even if she is not content, she sure does look good.

My friend, I said all that to say this. If all your joy and happiness rest upon the image you feel you must project and the equally dangerous problem-free life that you perceive others live, you will be miserable.

There must be a way that we as Christian leaders, wives, mothers and servants of the Lord can communicate to a world that relies solely upon image. How do we field this land mine today?

With hands raised to heaven worshiping God and tears streaming down my face, I sing words like, "Christ in me, the hope of glory, changing me from glory to glory, I want Your image to be seen in me." As soon as worship is over, out comes the Kleenex, compact and mirror to cover the little trails the tears made on my face. With lipstick reapplied, every trace of being totally exposed and wholly open before God is now instantly covered by my new makeup, which, incidentally, was being promoted by a ten-year-old model/actress on television.

Have you ever had one of those encounters with God that literally changed the direction and course of your life? We all have several moments in time when God made Himself so real that we will never forget it and never tire of telling it. The reason I care so deeply for young people and children is because of the pattern I see in God's Word concerning His timing in calling choice servants at an early age.

RECOVERY FROM
A HIGH SCHOOL NIGHTMARE

Ninth grade was a nightmare for me. My precious parents were pioneering a new Pentecostal church in a predominately Lutheran, Brethren/Amish area of Pennsylvania. My best friend of four years had, without cause or explanation, rejected me. I was alone in my first year of high school. Add to the experience a senior bully who would taunt me with slings and arrows. I simply did not understand.

"Holy Roller" is what my nemesis would cry out. I had no idea what in the world she was talking about, but her words made the other kids laugh at me. Walking down the hall, sitting in study hall, even in the bleachers during a football game, she was there.

I will never forget how she made me feel the day I wore a new outfit my mom had saved for two months to buy me for my fourteenth birthday. She ordered it

131

from the Poplar Club. My dear mother had sold catalog orders on the side to buy me my dream outfit. It
was beautiful, gray wool hip-huggers and a matching
gray, cream and yellow double-breasted blazer.
Trendy, expensive clothes were rare and memorable.
Like most parents, mine worked hard, and every
sacrifice was made so that our image of God was not
that of a *taker* but of a *rewarder.*

Proudly walking into the auditorium that night in
my new outfit, I spotted her. It was as though the devil
had whispered in her ear, "Here comes Cathy Rothert.
It's time to torment her."

Sure enough, she yelled across the building, "Cathy
Rothert. Holy Roller, so fat she has to roll down the
aisle." Now when you are fourteen, you have a zillion
different emotions that you do not think anyone else
has. The emotion that I felt at that moment was death
by mortification.

My new outfit, my long hair, which had been
straightened by rolling it in juice cans, and even my
white Nancy Sinatra boots all suddenly felt foolish. It
was as if I were trying too hard. I suddenly knew I would
never belong, much less lead, as I had desired to do.

Grabbing my brown suede shoulder bag, I ran, crying
all the way to the one-hundred-year-old house that
served as a parsonage across the street from the high
school. Next door stood the shadow of a half-finished
church building, which my father was endeavoring to
build, sometimes alone, while working an outside job.
There was the source of my torment, the eternal battle
to build.

I wanted to die the next day. I could just close my
eyes and go to sleep but was not allowed. The next day
was Saturday, and it was cleaning day. Strangely

132

enough, my mom did not give me the usual verbal list of chores. Because I had not given her my blow-by-blow account of the events of the night before, she sensed that all was not well.

Sobbing, I finally broke down, and with much embarrassment, I confessed my personal bully from hell to my mom. I literally saw no way out, no hope or no God who cared to save a little girl from the depression of loneliness, fear, guilt and shame.

Mom fell to the floor. There was no crisp, pink shirt-waisted dress or fluffy apron—there were bare knees on yellowed linoleum. No beautifully manicured red nails—only hands softened from washing, working and playing the piano. Those lovely hands were on my knees. Her voice was crying out to her God to intervene in the life of her child. Everything in her was battling a war I could not see. She would not lose me. A perfectly browned roast with potatoes might not be on the table that night, but there was the sloppy joes and a family around the table who honored God because we had come through a terrible battle that day.

My mom and dad continued to pray. I would hear them when they finally turned their lights out. Dad would always say to me, "Honey, you pray."

I am not sure how Doris Day's children turned out. Aunt Bea was a fantasy in Mayberry, a city of fantasy, but I know how Clive and Rose Rothert's kids turned out—not too bad. My brother still will not put that blue coat on and does not have enough hair for a John-John "do." Besides, he is a Navy officer.

The next month Dad encouraged me to try out for the chorus in the school musical *South Pacific*. God had heard my parent's prayers. I got the lead, a first for an underclassman. My Lord was restoring my self-image and giving me a little shot of courage and faith. High school became a joy. Those days of despair never returned, but I never forgot how vicious and cruel the enemy can be.

MY TORMENTOR WAS NOT WHO SHE HAD SEEMED TO BE

A funny thing happened in my junior year of high school. Once again Mom was selling stuff. It was the early seventies, and home parties were the rage. At this time she was selling Dutch-Maid clothes, which included underwear and pajamas. The demonstrator had evaded our living room with metal racks filled with wearing apparel. I had helped make cookies. Now the demonstrator, my mom and I were waiting for the invitees to arrive.

It was almost over when a woman knocked on our front door. I jumped up to open it and was relieved for the demonstrator's sake that someone had come. What I saw next will stay with me forever. Behind the woman, whom mom introduced as her friend from work (as opposed to her friend from church, the only people she knew), stood my tormentor!

"Rose, this is my daughter, the demon seed." Well, she did not actually say that.

My mother's friend then began what had to be the sweetest revenge ever invented in Motter School. She held up underpants to check for size on the front of this big girl—in my living room and in public. The girl was silent, solemn and did not seem to recognize me at all.

After they left, my mom told me that she had been praying for her friend's daughter. Dropping out of school, the girl had been sent away for rebellion and severe emotional problems. My tormentor had become human right before my eyes. Even at sixteen, I knew it was not a victory but a sad aside to this girl's young life. Things are never what they seem, and I want to encourage you not to despair.

Is that not why we all need Jesus so much? He takes an imperfect world and applies a perfect solution. We have been given an enormous capacity to forgive people and give them another chance.

PERMANENT?

All that is really permanent is God. His work is infallible, and His promises are unfailing. I still struggle with image today. When will it all end? I will let you know in forty-six more years.

125

Chapter 10

MARVELOUS, FABULOUS AND OTHER LIES

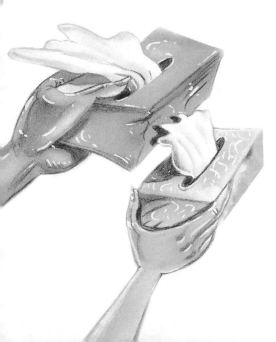

Cat walks three days, takes a train, has exact change for the subway, finds master three thousand miles away at the same convenience store where she was accidentally left during a family vacation seven years ago." This is followed by the words *amazing, miraculous, a true wonder.*

Maybe she really got left. Or maybe, just maybe, Mom got sick of Susie's new kitty Huntress, who waited until the family had company to drop a four-day-old, dead, headless bird on the visiting pastor's plate during dinner.

The next day Huntress went for a ride with the family. Then kitty mysteriously takes a seven-year field trip. She had been living between the Rice-A-Roni and the fake crab sections at the mini-mart.

A reporter asks Mrs. Thompson F. Johanasburg Lipitor, "What was your reaction when you found Huntress?"

Through clinched teeth, Mrs. Lipitor smiled as tears welled up in her eyes. Subconsciously she was remembering the dead bird incident. "Yes, miraculous, amazing." Her voice trails off.

We use various words to describe the most mundane facts—words like *amazing, wondrous, awesome.* The very fact that we found a parking space in front of the supermarket so we didn't have to walk two feet merits an *incredible.* When we arrive at the church on time with both earrings intact, it brings forth a *phenomenal.* I am not downplaying life's little miracles, but we have no words left for the truly spectacular.

In my devotions this morning, I read a fabulous biblical account that I have read so many times. But today I really needed it—AMAZING! It's the account of

Moses telling God that he thinks God is really over His head now:

> And Moses said, The people, among whom I am, are six hundred thousand men footmen; and thou hast said, I will give them flesh, that they may eat a whole month. Shall the flocks and the herds be slain for them, to suffice them? or shall all the fish of the sea be gathered together for them to suffice them?
>
> —NUMBERS 11:21–22, KJV

Now if I were Moses' mom, and he was talking to me in that smart tone, I probably would have smacked him. Basically he was telling *God* that there was no way He could feed all those people *and* in the allotted time.

If you read the preceding verses, you will discover the reason God was giving them thirty days of meat— it was because the people were crying, complaining and feeling sorry for themselves. The audacity of standing in God's face and telling Him that, with all due respect, nothing short of a miracle could fulfill God's word—like a miracle where the chickens plucked themselves and jumped into the oven, the cows lay down on hamburger buns and the fish melted their own butter for sautéing.

But wait a minute! That's what I had been doing— crying, complaining and feeling sorry for myself! God didn't come down and verbally speak to me about it, but He doesn't have to—I have His Word. Like the children of Israel, I also have my testimony. It is a great battle weapon if we will only use it.

My case was a terrible mistake. The person responsible for our accounting—including seeing that our car payments get made—was no longer in our employ. In sorting out the financial mess left behind, we discovered that Jerusha's car payment had been overlooked.

GOD DIDN'T COME DOWN AND VERBALLY SPEAK TO ME ABOUT IT, BUT HE DOESN'T HAVE TO—I HAVE HIS WORD.

When the phone call came that a truck had been dispatched to pick up the car for nonpayment, I was mortified. Thinking it was some sort of mistake, I began arguing with the person. I found out that repo people are not funny or flexible human beings. I personally think they are rather "jumpy" from being shot at too many times.

Begging for just a few minutes to sort out this whole mess, I uttered clichés like "I'm sure your computer made a mistake" and "Are you sure all the payments have been posted?"

I immediately contacted the Ford Motor Credit company, only to find out that the car payments were indeed in default. Well...our former bookkeeper was soon made aware of how serious the situation was. I yelled, pounded my fists, cried and railed, supposing that would help. I turned my anger up like two high-voltage laser lights to burn out the brains of any and all who could do this to us.

That was an attractive response, don't you think? Wouldn't TBN have loved to see me having a meltdown that would make the *Wizard of Oz* look like *Sesame Street.*

I was a one-woman "Hell's Gates and Death's Flames"—a live performance.

However, the Word clearly teaches us that man's anger doesn't work the righteousness of God. And God knows I've tried. I had to face the inevitable, horrible truth. There was absolutely nothing I could do to fix my situation!

I remembered something Bob Mumford had written at thirty years of age: "If God fixes a fix to fix you, just fix the fix that God fixed to fix you. It's all right. He'll just fix another fix—and He *will* fix you."

"PRAISE ME NOW"

I knelt down on the floor, or to be more accurate, I *threw* myself on the floor and began to sob heavily. Then I heard, *"Praise Me."*

I recognized that still, small familiar voice. Again I heard, *"Praise Me."* The fourth time the command was stronger and more demanding. Yet, in all honesty, in my heart I felt there was nothing to praise God for. I had been wounded by someone whom I dearly loved. My credit had been ruined, and a car that was close to being paid off was going to be taken away forcibly.

It's pretty hard to keep telling someone how wonderful that person is and remain angry. The Father has instituted praise as the vehicle to change our perspective instantly from *hopelessness* to *hopefulness.* When we start praising God, within minutes we are transformed

131

out of our self-centered, problem-plagued "it's-not-fair" victim mentalities.

THE FATHER HAS INSTITUTED PRAISE AS THE VEHICLE TO CHANGE OUR PERSPECTIVE INSTANTLY FROM HOPELESSNESS TO HOPEFULNESS.

Praise changes the perspective from your eyes to God's eyes. Somehow, by turning away from the *problem* to *praise*, we no longer feel responsible for having all the answers.

132

Lost in Praise

When I responded to God's instruction and became lost in praise to my Lord, it wasn't long until I felt totally lifted. It seemed as if I were transported to that special "secret place." It is not a physical place, but it is somewhere you can go to get away from the pressures of life and what sometimes seems like the unfairness of life.

It was providential, and no one can convince me otherwise. *Prison to Praise*, a slim volume of testimony by Merlin Carothers, was lying on my lap. My face was covered with tears. It was 1975, and my fiancé had just broken up with me. I was eighteen years old and just knew I would never love again, at least not like this. I held the small volume of testimony up to my eyes. Never had I read words like this. The concept of loving, praying for and actually thanking God for something or someone when I had been deliberately wounded—or in my case, my heart broken—was hard to grasp.

It was early morning, and there was a chill in the air. To me it was a sign that the night was over even though it was still dark outside. It just smelled like morning. I remember walking from the parsonage where I lived with my family, unlocking the church side door and falling on my face at the altar.

I raised my hands and opened my mouth to speak, but nothing came out. I remember it so clearly because it was the day I came to know the heart and character of my God.

That morning I learned a lesson many believers never learn, or if they do, they don't embrace it. It's total, absolute, unquestionable trust in HIM. That trust becomes manifested in loud, abandoned, uninhibited, continuous praise!

133

I cried, laughed, sang and rejoiced until the afternoon sun streamed through the church's stained-glass window. I now know the meaning of the last verse of that old song "In the Garden."

> I'd stay in the garden with Him
> Tho' the night around me be falling;
> But He bids me go; thro' the voice of woe,
> His voice to me is calling.*

I guess His voice is one of woe because after we finally get to that place of loud, abandoned, uninhibited, continuous praise, He knows it might be years before we come back there. For some, it will take the catalyst of crisis for us to be abandoned enough. That place is not simple prayer—it's much, much more than that. It's enjoyment!

It's a place of pure joy, total trust, great contentment, a ceasing from strife, a place where we choose not to worry any more. I believe that many who are on drugs are looking for that kind of a "high," but the closest the world has to offer often brings an overdose and death. They are looking in the wrong place.

A year after that early morning praise experience, I walked down the aisle with God's best. He would be my knight in shining armor, a man who loved God more than me (gasp)! He is my senior in the things of the Spirit and a true high priest in our home.

Twenty-five years later I am still grateful to God that "my choice" walked out of my life, even though at that time I thought it unbelievably cruel of God to let that happen to me.

Like Moses, we should become much more understanding, more savvy in the ways of the Lord and much more astute in the dealings of the Spirit. If God tells us that there will be meat for a month for six hundred thousand men, our attitude should be, "No problem!"

We've been through this before, and we know our God doesn't play with us. When He speaks, He calls those things of which He speaks into existence. But unless we have been spending time in our "secret place," it is impossible for our natural mind to just believe and accept what He speaks.

Awesome, incredible, amazing, great, glorious, miraculous—those words belong to Him.

A WORD FROM THE LORD

Beloved one! You said, "God, my Lord, where are You? Do You care? Do You care that I am

TOTAL, ABSOLUTE, UNQUESTIONABLE TRUST IN HIM IS MANIFESTED IN LOUD, ABANDONED, UNINHIBITED CONTINUOUS PRAISE.

hurting? Does it matter to heaven that I have been suffering? Where, my God, is my answer? Where, great Deliverer, is Your justice?"

135

My child, do not abandon the desert in which you have found yourself. I will meet you in the empty place; only let Me come in.

Open your heart and your spirit to Me. You are not alone. Even though you may not understand why everything has happened, very shortly you will see My hand of deliverance. Last year was one of trials, tribulations and testing. But this year will be one of answers and solutions.

You have read My Word, "Having done all—stand." It is Me, the Mighty One who gives you the grace to stand. I will shorten the length of "standing time" so you will see My goodness in the land of the living. Just a little while, just a

LIKE MOSES, WE SHOULD BECOME MUCH MORE UNDERSTANDING, MORE SAVVY IN THE WAYS OF THE LORD AND MUCH MORE ASTUTE IN THE DEALINGS OF THE SPIRIT.

short time, and victory will come. REJOICE, REJOICE! Heaven is already starting to party! My first choice is on the way!

---

*"In the Garden" by C. Austin Miles. Public domain.

Chapter 11

IF YOU'RE NOT DEAD—START REJOICIN'

I was late—again. Actually, I was right on time, but this was the United States Navy. Therefore, I was late. And don't bother showing the officer on duty the wall clock, your watch, time and temperature on the phone or *his* watch—you are late!

My brother Harold Randall (we call him *Randy*, his Navy pals call him *Hal*) was retiring from the Navy after twenty-three years of service, and they were having a military celebration to mark the occasion. One of the ceremonial events that touched my heart was when the commander called a group of men and women in full uniform to form a line down the center aisle. They began with the lowest rank at the far end, graduating to the next rank and so on, ending with my brother at the head of the line.

As the music began to play, a folded flag that had been carried on a Blue Angels' jet was held by the lowest-ranking seaman. He saluted the flag and then very ceremoniously passed it on to the next sailor. After going through nine pairs of hands, it was handed to my brother. I learned later that each sailor represented one of the ranks my brother had achieved—up to his present rank, that of lieutenant.

Randy joined the Navy at seventeen years of age, right out of high school. He seemed so sad and lonely and little the day my mom and dad drove him to Miami to join his unit and begin his new life. Married at twenty, he had to leave his bride and go to sea for seven months. His letters home were mixed with excitement and sadness as he began to count down the months, weeks and days until he could return home.

It wasn't long after returning that my brother saw that

the only way he could excel and be promoted was to go to college. For eight years he would come home from the base, gather his books and go to school. Four nights

WHEN WE COME INTO THE KINGDOM OF GOD, IT'S FOR LIFE.

a week and weekends he would sacrifice for the goal. By the time he finished he had two children, therefore squeezing in his studies between piano lessons, soccer practice, homework and church.

With his wife's encouragement, he applied for Officer Candidate School, was selected and again left home, family and his familiar routine to pursue his goal. He went on to get his master's degree, which meant more school nights and studying. In addition to that, he received several promotions as his commanding officers recognized his devotion to his job and country.

Now it was his choice to leave the Navy in order to pursue another career. In the interim, he chose to make two trips to Third World countries to take medical supplies to them and tell them about Jesus.

As the sailors in that ceremonial line passed the flag at his retirement service, I could clearly see God's pattern for His servants. Some sign up, and others are drafted, but every individual is responsible for how far they excel.

I know my brother wanted to quit many times. The separations from his family meant God-forsaken duty stations, but he stayed, believing always that somehow his efforts would be rewarded. The Navy took him all over the world, told him what to wear and where to live.

I know of men and women who join the military service with rose-colored glasses, expecting their service days will be a bed—or should I say a berth?—of roses. Yet when the military becomes more than flags, uniforms and ceremonial marching, they quit.

When we come into the kingdom of God, it's for life. If you have a goal, a vision and destiny, you can believe that there will be sacrifices.

Each rank my brother held represented additional training, greater diligence, deeper commitment to the service and a financial obligation. This was not required by the service. My brother saw what was available to him and went after it. The promotions did not come overnight, and he did not always get every rank, promotion, job or duty station he sought after. I watched him make many sacrifices to attain his goal.

Being someone who always tends to see the spiritual side of things, I found that all the parts of my brother's military ceremony, as well as his life leading up to this occasion, could be applied to the Christian's walk with the Lord. Yes, there are many sacrifices, but we continue to strive to attain our goal.

I am often reminded that there is a lot more *gore* than *glory* in ministry. God has blessed me graciously and, I might add, mysteriously anointed me. Sometimes I feel like paying the price, but there are other times I want to have the option of going to church or spending the weekend with my kids.

There are obvious sacrifices that people in ministry must make. But there are also the things most people

142

never even think about. For you, dear reader, I am about to spill my guts to you about the intimacy of ministry, traveling ministry and women in ministry.

I AM OFTEN REMINDED THAT THERE IS A LOT MORE GORE THAN GLORY IN MINISTRY.

HAIRCUTS ON THE ROAD

"You ought to let me cut and highlight your hair." I heard the voice over my shoulder. When I turned around, my eyes had to look down about two feet to find the source of the offer, one that came with a long, southern drawl.

"Hi, my name is Hepsiba (that's in the Bible). I do hair. I do pastor's hair, Associate Minister Calvin's hair and Administrator/Apostle Johnson's hair. Now he's actually bald, but I put a thick, all natural beeswax with retina on his hair, and then I pull it through a rice paper sorta hat. We rinse it, blow it, dry it, and then I take those seven thickened strands and do a back-combing. It looks so natural, nobody says a word about his baldness." Through all this exhortation, Hepsiba has not taken a breath.

Well, I thought, *I actually do need a trim.* And my father was always confused because I told him that I dyed my blonde roots brown every eight weeks. I don't think he bought it, really.

143

Hepsiba happened to have some time that very day, so I thanked her profusely and got directions to her shop. I was about to learn one of the Holy Spirit's greatest lessons concerning ignoring His still, small voice. Actually, it was my still, small voice that was screaming, jumping up and down, holding its throat in a mocking

GIVE YOUR HAIR—AND YOUR SPIRITUAL LIFE— JUST WHAT IT NEEDS TO THRIVE.

chokehold, falling over while kicking his legs. Looking back, I now see that my inner man was really, really trying to tell me something. I just thought maybe Hepsiba needed ministry. Perhaps she was simply demon possessed, and God was sending me to deliver her.

To her credit, my daughter tried to stop me. She respectfully pointed out that there was no one...I mean no one else in the hair salon. The telephone never rang the entire time we were there. Hepsiba had to go to the drug store to buy a hair coloring kit. There was dust on the appointment book. I pointed out that perhaps the dust was simply a light covering of recently cut hair. Then my spirit man started singing, "It Is Well With My Soul."

Hepsiba sat me in her chair, shook out an old, dye-stained cape and threw it around me. Grabbing pieces of my hair she muttered, "Mmm," followed by, "Well, it's only hair. I'll be right back, don't go anywhere."

"Run," cried my little inner man. "Run! Remember Samson; remember Absalom."

As I waited for Hepsiba to return from the back room where she had disappeared with her discount drugstore bag, I noticed the poster on the salon wall. All the models were African American with newly styled, shiny Afros. Diana Ross, Shaft and Shirley Caeser were all smiling and modeling the newest, most modern style—for 1971—a long time ago.

"I've never done Caucasian hair, but it can't be that different. I just want to bless the Lord's servant," said little Hepsiba. She then proceeded to give me what I found out later was a Jheri-curl. Let's just say it was the last Jheri-curl I'm ever going to have.

One of our daughters is African American and four are biracial. My hair doesn't resemble theirs at all. I have my Aunt Minnie's hair.

All heads of hair are not alike. I think even Hepsiba knows that today. At our house we have a cabinet full of pink oil, Nature's Shampoo, Pert, Head and Shoulders—plus the stuff that's supposed to make you taller, thinner and immensely attractive just from shampooing your hair. And each of us uses the bottle that is best for our hair. Give your hair—and your spiritual life—just what it needs to thrive.

145

"I'M ONLY THREE CLASSES AWAY FROM MY LICENSE"

That's what the massage therapist said to me at the ladies conference. Even her pastor's wife assured me that this girl has remarkable hands, even though she personally had never had a massage.

Three and one-half hours later, she had given me a

full-body massage. I got up from her new massage bed, which still smelled like plastic, and threw up. I

WE SAY WE WANT TO APPEAR GENEROUS, GRATEFUL, SPIRITUAL, CHRISTLIKE OR WHATEVER, BUT WE JUST DON'T WANT TO BE REJECTED.

know she meant well, but there must have been something in those last three classes that this gal needed to know. A great lesson came from that three-hour massage: "A little knowledge can be dangerous."

She had quite a bit of understanding of muscles— especially of those that hurt right away—and some giftings, including great compassion. That compassion is what got her into the field to begin with. But she hurt me. She meant well, but it took months before my neck stopped hurting.

There are so many precious people in churches along the way who want to help, want to stand out in the crowd. Many simply want to give back to you out of grateful, loving hearts.

Some are truly gifted, others horribly misguided. Why would I bother using these pages to share these stories? Well, the mark of a true teacher is that he or she can take something difficult and profound and make it simple.

My intentions for this chapter are certainly to make you laugh, and even forget for a little while the trials that you are facing. Laughter is medicine, good medicine. It goes deep into your bones and will restore you mentally, physically and emotionally.

If you're in ministry, perhaps you will see yourself in these pages and know that you are not alone. It's really not so bad. Whatever you go through for the gospel's sake counts. Suffering comes to each of us in different ways.

FACIALS THAT BURNED THE SKIN ON MY FACE

I remember well the photographer/makeup artist who made me look like a (with great respect to the bereaved) dead person. Would my skin ever recover?

Then there was the vitamin/mineral lady. And I remember the hostess who just wanted to swing me by her home for a minute so I could meet her family. The problem was, she was supposed to be taking me to the church service. This woman wanted me to minister to her husband and teenage children—who did not want ministry. They wouldn't come to the service, so she thought it was "God" who arranged for her to pick me up for the meeting.

Her husband and children were appalled that I was there and furious with their mother. She meant well, but she was not sensitive to the Holy Spirit. I was late for the meeting, and the pastor was understandably unhappy.

"Why didn't you just tell her no?" my husband

147

asked me when I got home and related the story. What a silly man!

"I was a captive, and she didn't exactly warn me, and, well…maybe God did want me to go…" I sort of trailed off. My excuses, when aired, sounded pitiful.

THE BRIGHTER YOU GET THE MORE BUGS YOU ATTRACT.

It's the same reason we buy half a frozen cow out of someone's trunk, open a charge account we don't need when the salesgirl's eyes begin to water or buy all the new makeup (and brushes) they put on us during the free makeover. All the time we know we can't afford it and do not need it. So what is it?

I don't know. We say yes to magazine subscriptions and buy Girl Scout cookies when we already bought six boxes of the same thing from the other neighbor's daughter. One can never have enough thin mints!

Guilt! That's why I say yes when I mean no. After all, can you remember when you bought two to get one free, even though you didn't need the first one? Well, I can always give it to so-and-so for…(pick one: Christmas, birthday, missionary box or a present for the teacher).

We fear how we will look to other people if we say no. We say we want to appear generous, grateful, spiritual, Christlike or whatever, but we just don't want to be rejected.

My dear family continually tells me, "Cathy, please

148

don't say yes and then have us cancel later when you don't want to go."

I know, I know. We need the Lord to help us speak the truth. When the Lord speaks to me, telling me to say yes or no, and I don't obey, that's a lie. But it is also offensive to my Lord for me to say what people want to hear—if it's not also what the Father is saying.

Do you remember the biblical account of the old prophet and the young prophet in 1 Kings 13? That Bible story always confused me. Here was this older, seasoned, prophetic seer who had heard of the wonderful ministry of this young prophet. The old man set out to see this man who had done a really bold and fearless thing by standing up against the wicked king without fear for his own life.

Who was this brave young hero prophet? The old man needed to find out. There is always a cry in the land from a fresh voice, one who is uncompromising, one who cannot be bought; someone who would willingly lay down his life for the king, his people and for righteousness.

When the old prophet found him, he asked him to come to his house for a meal and a drink and some fellowship. The young man refused, having been directed by God not to stop to take refreshment or to return the way he came—two simple commands from God. At some point the old prophet knew of these commands. The old prophet knew the boy needed to obey precisely and immediately. It was a test worthy of an up-and-coming major vessel of God.

The old prophet lied by saying, "But God told me you were to come home with me and eat." (See 1 Kings 13:18.) Would the young man stand firm to God's exact instructions? What made the young prophet disregard

149

His command? Did he fear what the old prophet would say? Was he afraid of being rejected?

While still in the early part of his ministry, he was found to be only partially faithful—which is to be unfaithful. His unfaithfulness brought on his demise.

Not fair may be your cry!

But the brighter you get the more bugs you attract. It's not easy to take the criticism from those you love and honor in ministry. After a rebuke from a friend, I was licking my wounds. Bishop Bill Hamon's wife, Evelyn—"Mom" Hamon—said, "Well, Cathy, they said you would be reviled and even be killed. You're not dead yet, so rejoice."

So I say to you:

> You're not dead—so stop crying and rejoice!

CHAPTER 12

STRESSED IS JUST DESSERTS SPELLED BACKWARDS

Did you ever have a morning that turned into a day that eventually became an unending wilderness? You know, no matter how you opened the matchbox, it was upside down all day! Stress is a part of our lives today. I speak from experience. Just try writing a book.

When I was a kid, I thought my parents were unbelievably cruel. They were also sneaky. In my warped little pea brain, I thought they had incredibly cushy lives. Imagine going to work all day, getting to drive a car, eat whatever for lunch, come home and be the boss of the television. After all, we only had one. I probably needed inner healing.

Whereas, *I* had to go to school. I spent hours in futility learning worthless principles like addition, spelling and finding the sum of the total of the area of a parallelogram. After all, the world was beckoning me.

Later in life, sitting at my dreary bank teller job and juggling college classes when I could afford them and had the time and will to attend, I looked back on my childhood perception and laughed. HA! How foolish was I? After all, I was all of twenty-one years old now.

Now, no matter how difficult things have been over the years with the losses and heartaches, the Spirit of God inside of me is rising up in faith. No matter what situation I find myself in, God is teaching me to rejoice, which is why I love the prophetic ministry so very much. Prophetic ministry anchors itself in God's amazing mercy, the incredible Word and the ability to continually bring the word to pass. In fact, we offend His very nature when we limit the Holy One of Israel.

It has been said that man can live three months without food, three days without water, three minutes without air, but no more than three seconds without hope! The thing that sets Christians apart in life is that we are never without hope. The only way we can possibly live in this present age is "looking for the blessed hope and glorious appearing of our great God and Savior Jesus Christ" (Titus 2:13).

When I was drowning in a sea of grief over the death of my beloved father, the only way I could be rescued was to cling to 1 Thessalonians 4:13. It says, "But I do not want you to be ignorant, brethren, concerning those who have fallen asleep, lest you sorrow as others who have no hope."

A decision was set before me either to grasp the Preserver of life, or to let the sea swell of grief kill me. Knowing our future is what keeps us from grieving, "as do the rest that have no hope."

Hope is a facade to those who do not know the Lord. God will not abandon His people. Though we are faithless at times, He will still be faithful to us. In a day yet to come, God will fulfill every promise He has ever made.

155

Not even Jesus was immune to the suffering and loss that we face. I have heard the modern-day teaching that was twisted from the original word of faith. The basic perverted message stated, "If something goes wrong in your life, and if you have a problem, it is due to either unconfessed sin or a lack of faith." While this may be true in some instances, Jesus was not only sinless but had pure faith—and went straight into the wilderness because of it.

We are disillusioned when we believe that every action brings either a swift phenomenal reward or a horrible immediate retribution. This very unbiblical way of thinking will leave you discouraged, mad at yourself and God and pretty much mad at everyone. If you do everything perfectly faithful to the Word and live a flawless life under a microscope, you will still go through the wilderness.

Will He Find Faith?

Imagine for a moment that we are with Jesus on a hill-side and listening to Him preach. Since this *is* my book, imagine that because of our stellar Christian lifestyle we are with the "in group," which gives us the privilege of front-row seats and very special VIP crusade passes.

After a rousing chorus of "How Great Thou Art," Jesus quiets the crowd and George Beverly Shea blesses us and says, "Hey, He's been around a long, long time." The crowd then gets quiet. A spotlight comes up and Jesus begins to teach.

He begins by asking His followers a very interesting question, one He probably already knows the answer to. The question asked is, "When I return, will I find faith?"

Now I have been waiting for six hours in the blazing sun to get VIP seating, so I can assure you that I am slightly crabby. In response to Jesus' question, I begin snorting while shrugging my shoulders and snickering under my breath. Looking over at Peter, or possibly Judas, whom I doubtless would have chosen as my two dearest friends, I begin to chortle.

Will He find faith? Is He talking to me? Is He talking to *me?* You have got to be kidding. I am the Sicilian disciple, the Robert DeNiro disciple.

"Faith, Lord? You wanna talk faith? I know I got faith!" I yell. At that point, Luke the physician would have quietly slipped behind me and given me an injection so that Jesus could continue His sermon.

Jesus knew that the pressure of the age in which we live would tax the foundation of every principle and code of faith on which we base our lives. Who has not lost loved ones after tirelessly praying in faith? Some people, even those who believed with all that is within them, still did not get the job, the promotion or the healing.

My Message Paled Before This Vietnamese Man

Just before I was to minister at a leadership conference in Tacoma, Washington, the pastor of the host church, Kevin Gerall, told the gathered crowd that a pastor from Vietnam would share for five minutes before my message.

My Bible and notebook contained my carefully designed message, which was anxiously sitting on my lap. I loved this pastor and his church and wanted to deliver an awesome word that would make them glad they had invited me.

157

The young pastor from Vietnam began to thank us for coming to his country with M-16s to fight and for laying down American lives for their political freedom. "But several years ago," he said to us, "you came back with a one-way ticket and John 3:16 to deliver to us spiritually."

As he talked about his imprisonment, beatings, deprivation and the capture of his young pregnant wife, my sermon started shrinking in the notebook, along with my ego. We sat and wept. We wept for our shallowness and repented for the complaining we did over practically nothing. In the person of an unknown

Vietnamese man we witnessed true leadership.

When Pastor Kevin formally introduced me, I just sat there. But after his words, we spontaneously jumped to our feet to applaud this humble man who had risked his life over and over again for his Jesus. My idea of suffering is getting my hair pulled through a frosting cap, but this man was so pure and motivated by love.

Jesus was led into the wilderness to be tempted by Satan following His greatest victory. I would have been insulted. Why would God repay my faithfulness with a valley? But the act was not *punishment*—it was *promotion*.

PSALM 23 IS A ROAD MAP FOR THE LIVING

Psalm 23, a psalm of David, is read at funerals more than any other scriptures, even for funerals of unbelievers. However, Psalm 23 is not for the dead—it is a road map for the living. Strap on your safety belt because here we go! If you carefully read the next few paragraphs, they will change your life.

Psalm 23:1 states, "The LORD is my shepherd; I shall not want." When Jesus called us His sheep, it was not a compliment, because sheep are some of the dumbest animals in the world. The shepherd needs us to see that He not only has a corporate relationship with us as a flock, but He also has a personal relationship with us individually. We have no need to want. Everything that we need is provided to us on a daily basis. Stop worrying about tomorrow!

Psalm 23:2 continues by saying, "He leads me beside the still waters." Did you know that sheep are afraid of the sound of running water? Even if a sheep has eaten and is thirsty, it will go with its thirst unquenched because the water frightens sheep, and they will run from it.

As a new Christian, my husband had an insatiable appetite for the things of God. Driving down the road one night shortly after he had gotten saved, he saw a church with its lights on and cars in the parking lot. It was Monday night, and the sign outside proclaimed "Revival." He was so impressed that people would be in church on a Monday night that he parked his car, went inside and sat in the back row.

This church was a completely alien world to him. He was raised in a military officer's home. Along with that, his father was Jewish. Just receiving Jesus was an unbelievable event that would change the course of his life.

Sitting in the back of this Pentecostal Holiness Church, he saw things that his analytical mind could not understand. When the visiting evangelist asked who wanted more of the Holy Ghost, my babe-in-the-spiritual-woods husband was the only one to come down to the front.

159

Immediately twenty pairs of hands were on his head, chest, arms and shoulders, shaking, yelling and praying down all of heaven. He fell to the floor, not under the power of the Spirit, but under the power of Martian Christians. After finding a hole between the many legs, he crawled out on his hands and knees through the crowd. Not looking back, he promised God never to return. He was scared—the sound of the "running water" had frightened him.

Just a few days later, he was invited by a friend to a gathering of Charismatic Christians. While at the service, he simply and quietly received the indwelling of the Holy Spirit, and his life began another new course.

Psalm 23:3 says, "He restores my soul; He leads me in the paths of righteousness for His name's sake." The little phrase "restores my soul" does not mean that the Father sends angels to sing slow, dismal songs until we are refreshed. Instead, the phrase literally means, "He changes my image because His Name is on me."

It happened in Dillard's department store. First the saleswoman ignored me and treated me as though I were an indigent leper. I will admit that I looked a little "rough," but after all, I do have seven kids. I am not sure if it was my drowned-rat hair that was desperately in need of attention or the mustard and various, mysterious food stains that decorated my shirt. Hey, it *did* have a polo pony embroidered on my breast pocket.

Anyway, after her third rude comment of, "I'm not sure we carry that in your size. We only go up to XXL in this department," I wanted to say something rude so badly. The taste of acid was dripping from my mouth. After all, just because I am a Christian does not mean that I am a doormat.

With my mouth open and snotty retort ready to rip, I heard an angelic voice behind me say, "Cathy Lechner? Do you remember me? I was in your meeting eighteen months ago. You called me out, prayed for me and told me that God was giving my husband and me a baby. We had been trying for five years." She then pulled back the receiving blanket to show me the five-month-old baby sleeping in the new stroller.

With joyous pride that only a new mother knows, she said, "Mrs. Lechner, this is Dylan." Mom was starting to weep. All the blustering anger toward the saleslady left as I changed gears in front of this precious picture.

160

The Holy Spirit saved me from opening my mouth and letting the entire world see my unsanctified flesh.

God saves us and then spends a lifetime changing our image because His name is on us. It is the reason we cringe when we hear that our child got detention for poking the teacher with her pointer stick. The truth of the matter is that our child is a reflection of us, a reflection of our character, our discipline and our manners.

What image of God do people see when they watch you? As they hear you speak, what do your friends and family hear about the kind of Father you have?

SPIRITUAL VALLEYS

Psalm 23:4 says, "Yea, though I walk through the valley of the shadow of death, I will fear no evil." My friend, the valley of the Lord has only one purpose in your life. You can bind it away, confess it away, plead, beg and declare that it does not exist, but you will still be faced with the valley.

How do you know if you are in a valley? Well, the valley is the place where your favorite scripture verse does not thrill you. In addition, it is when your best friend, who always has a word for you even when you do not want one, is on vacation. Everything is dry, and there are no visible signs of life anywhere. The valley is the place where you feel as if you're going to die. Being in the valley is painful and lonely, and we want a word with a release date.

Some Christians who spend so much time in the valley think valley life is the same as normal Christian life. They live, for the most part, depressed, worried, fearful and joyless. Those precious but deluded saints always live in the future, and believe that God's

161

promises are for the future. To them, prosperity and blessing will come after the Rapture, or just slightly before. I am sure that you know the sermon from memory that admonishes Christians to *walk through* the valley, not *camp in* it. Once we learn the lesson of the valley we can move on, and the devil will not be able to throw you off course anymore. The trip through the valley will never get any shorter if we sit down and cry.

Psalm 23:4 also declares, "Your rod and Your staff, they comfort me." A sheep has a one-track mind. He puts his head down and keeps moving forward, eating as he goes. They have been known to eat themselves off the side of a mountain and take a part of the flock with them. For that reason, the shepherd has a rod and staff.

We have all seen the Christmas picture of the shepherd with a long pole and a hook at the end. The hook is used to grab errant sheep and pull them back physically from the edge of disaster. Did you know that at the other end of the hook is a knotty piece of carved wood in the shape of a ball?

If a "Judas" sheep continues to rebel and eat its way to death, the shepherd will gather it up in his arms and use the knotty end of the rod to break the sheep's back leg. He will then set and dress the leg and hoist the sheep up over his shoulders. That sheep will stay on the shepherd's neck every day as the leg heals. All the while that sheep hears his master's voice continuously while healing. Once the process of mending is finished, the "Judas" sheep now knows the voice of his master. Soon he becomes the lead sheep and an incredible help to his master.

Now, before you grab for your pen and paper to write me a nasty letter rebuking me for even implying that our great Shepherd would ever hurt or much less break your leg, hold on and save your stamp. Have you ever said, "I'm disciplining you because I love you"? Part of our walk with God includes His discipline, as distasteful as it can be.

Here is a small nugget for any reader who has gotten to this chapter. I have been writing just about this entire manuscript lying down on various beds—my bed, motel beds or anywhere I can get flat and rest my back. No, God did not afflict me. It is a combination of life on the road ministering and being in hotels and airplanes every weekend. It is also because the enemy took advantage of a fall and now seeks to incapacitate me.

By God's grace, I continue to go. However, I do try to rest in between. Lying on your back gives you a great deal of time to talk to Jesus, to hear His voice and to become stronger. His rod and staff comfort me because they save my life. When I am ignorant, He saves me with the staff. When I am willfully disobedient, He spares me with His rod.

Psalm 23:5 says, "You prepare a table before me in the presence of my enemies." Human nature does not want you to sit down and eat until all enemies have been vanquished.

163

In Sicilian families, a good hostess never sits down. She is refilling bowls, heating the sauce, adding meatballs and getting drinks. Many times my mom or my nana would not even have a plate set for themselves on the table. However, in God's house, the proof that you have learned the lesson of the valley, which is to fear no evil, is that you must sit down to dinner. Believe me, your enemies will be raging around you. While car payments, rebellious kids, ministry obligations, work and just plain life are still raging, you must sit down at the feast prepared for you and then eat!

Anorexics, a malady I have never been accused of having, starve their bodies of food out of a root of fear of being out of control, fear of being fat and fear of rejection. This fear will eventually cause a poor soul in its grip to deny all food, resulting in death.

Are you spiritually anorexic? Are you fearful, running here and there, on the phone, having meetings, checking e-mail, voice mail and the U. S. mail? If you do not eat, you will die. Can you force yourself to sit at the table and eat slowly while the enemy is raging all around? Can you enjoy it, and even ask for another helping?

The Anointing

The same scripture continues by saying, "You anoint my head with oil; my cup runs over." Notice that the anointing does not come until I learn the lesson of the valley. I can eat with gusto while all of hell rages around me and learn to enjoy His voice and presence. Then BAM! Kick it up another notch! The anointing with power comes for miracles. The word of knowledge, faith, prophecy and the clear, unmistakable voice of the Shepherd is heard because all obstacles are out of the way.

Hallelujah! It makes me want to shout. Imagine David, inspired by the Holy Spirit so long ago that he still speaks a sermon on sheep that is relevant to me today.

My Life's Lesson?

Surely goodness and mercy shall follow me all the days of my life; and I will dwell in the house of the LORD forever.

—PSALM 23:6

I knew a woman with two little apricot poodles named Goodness and Mercy. They were always at her feet and following her around. The blessings of goodness and mercy come after dessert. God's goodness and His faithfulness will follow you all your days. We get to dwell in "His House" forever. Not in heaven as we know it, but in His house—Daddy's house.

DADDY'S HOUSE

I end this book as I began, crying out to you to come home. Daddy's house is the best place to be. It is a place of acceptance. Sure, some of the family are weird; some are too loud, and some embarrass us. I have acquaintances who think they can sing, but they can't. Our Father loves them all. He loves us all the same.

For the Spirit of the Lord says:

> My daughter, do you think that I have forgotten My promise to you? I pledged My help and My assistance to you, and I will not fail.
>
> You will look back on this day and declare My faithfulness. For in a short time I will bring down the stronghold of My enemies, and we will shout together in victory.
>
> Do not turn back. Lift up your head. You are more precious to Me than you can imagine. So rest in Me, faint not, wait and I will give you breath and life. I will restore your joy. I will mend your house, and together they will rejoice.

DRY YOUR EYES AND GET READY TO PARTY

Throw your hands up in the air and start shouting. You only have to shout unto the Lord with the same intensity and volume you use when you shout at your husband, kids and the dog that has just made a woo-woo on your new carpet five minutes before your prayer group is to arrive.

Give God audible, loud, glorious words of thanks. Thank Him for the fresh water of His Spirit and for His Word. Thank Him for your "yucky" valley and for His faithfulness in your helplessness.

Confer on your God Father the place He longs to occupy. Do you understand? Kiss Him, the Head of the family. Hold Him close because His heart beats faster when He hears your voice.

He will lavish heaven on you, but do not just try it—*do it!* Do not become discouraged if you do not feel anything, and do not give up when you don't receive an instant answer.

Dry your eyes and get ready to party. You may keep your hanky, but please use it only for waving.

—In joy,
Cathy

If you enjoyed *I'm Tired of Crying, It's Time to Laugh Again*, here are some other Cathy Lechner titles from Charisma House that we think will minister to you...

I Hope God's Promises Come to Pass Before My Body Parts Go South
Cathy Lechner
ISBN: 0-88419-529-5
Retail Price: $11.99

With hilarious anecdotes and side-splitting stories, Cathy's anointed words will minister faith and hope to you—before your body parts go south.

I'm Trying to Sit at His Feet, but Who's Going to Cook Dinner?
Cathy Lechner
ISBN: 0-88419-409-4
Retail Price: $12.99

In the midst of your pressure situation, Cathy shows you how to walk in peace as God's Holy Spirit reveals His purposes for your life.

Couldn't We Just Kill 'em and Tell God They Died?
Cathy Lechner
ISBN: 0-88419-433-7
Retail Price: $12.99

Cathy's anointed words will minister hope and healing to your troubled relationships and help you to love the impossible people in your life.

You've Got to be Kidding, I Thought This Was the Great Tribulation!
Cathy Lechner
ISBN: 0-88419-667-4
Retail Price: $12.99

Trials and tribulation. Yes, the Lord promised that we would endure both before He returned. But Cathy Lechner wants you to know two things: 1) You're not alone, and 2) Expect God's deliverance soon!

 To pick up a copy of any of these titles, contact your local Christian bookstore or order online at www.charismawarehouse.com.